Karoo Ramblings

short stories & tall tales

*This book is dedicated to the memory of my father,
Norman Biggs, who loved the Karoo in all its
moods and instilled the same love in all his children.
Many of the stories in it are taken from his letters
and notes, which I have collected and read over and
over, with renewed delight at every reading.*

Many thanks to the following who helped with
valuable anecdotes, research and advice:

Gail Alswang, Alan Avis, Roger Biggs,
Belinda Gordon and Rose Willis

Karoo Ramblings

short stories & tall tales
by David Biggs

illustrations by Tony Grogan

First published in 2004 by Struik Publishers
(a division of New Holland Publishing (South Africa) (Pty) Ltd)
New Holland Publishing is a member of Johnnic Communications Ltd

Garfield House, 86–88 Edgware Road, London W2 2EA, United Kingdom
www.newhollandpublishers.com

80 McKenzie Street, Cape Town 8001, South Africa
www.struik.co.za

14 Aquatic Drive, Frenchs Forest, NSW 2086, Australia

218 Lake Road, Northcote, Auckland, New Zealand

Copyright © 2004 in published edition: Struik Publishers
Copyright © 2004 in text: David Biggs
Copyright © 2004 in illustrations: Struik Publishers

ISBN 1 86872 941 9

3 5 7 9 10 8 6 4 2

Publishing manager: Dominique le Roux
Managing editor: Lesley Hay-Whitton
Illustrator: Tony Grogan
Designer: Sean Robertson
Proofreader: Helen de Villiers

Reproduction by Hirt & Carter Cape (Pty) Ltd
Printed and bound in Cape Town by The Lithographic Co.

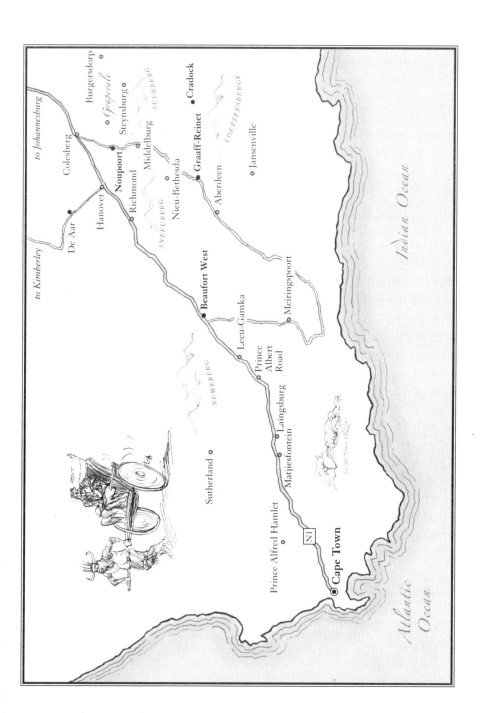

CONTENTS

Foreword

As they say at the beginning of real books: "Names and places have been changed to protect the innocent."

In this case names and places have probably been changed simply because I've forgotten the real ones. I make no claim to perfect accuracy. And, in any case, why let mere facts interfere with a good story? These are my memories – and in some cases the memories of members of my family – and memory can be a slippery little devil.

I remember a conversation I overheard in the Handelshuis supermarket in Middelburg once while I was waiting for my mother to finish her grocery shopping. It went something like this.

"What ever happened to that red-headed girl who worked in the chemist's shop? Remember her? What was her name? Rhoda, I think."

"No, it was Emma. I think her husband ran off with that doctor's wife."

"Ah yes, that's right, I remember now. But wasn't it the policeman's wife?"

"No, you're thinking of the Van Rensburg woman who went off with the magistrate. I'm pretty sure she was called Rhoda."

"But the Van Rensburg woman never worked for the chemist, did she?"

"No, she worked for the doctor. I think he married her after his wife ran off with that girl's husband."

"That's right. Wasn't she Emma?"

"No, she was Rhoda, as far as I remember. The policeman's wife was the one who died quite early. I think it was from a stroke."

"Was that before he went off with the Emma woman?"

My head was spinning when I finally picked up Mom's parcels.

But that's the way memory is.

The Karoo is obviously full of memories for many people. I've often been surprised by the reaction I get whenever I mention the Karoo in the daily "Tavern of the Seas" column I write for the *Cape Argus*. It seems that at least half the population of Cape Town grew up in the Karoo, or spent their most memorable school holidays with friends on a Karoo farm.

I'm told the word "Karoo" comes from an old Khoi word that means something like "dreadfully hot and dusty place". Hot and dusty it may be but, once it grips you by the heart, the Karoo never lets you go.

Sit down, pull up a coffee and share some of the stories with me in the shade of a handy peppercorn tree.

Notes from the Great Karoo

Many South Africans have, at one time or another, travelled the long, straight N1 highway that stretches from Cape Town all the way to Gauteng, the bustling economic heart of the country. For much of the route, the road runs through the great, endless plains of the grey Karoo. Small dusty towns like Colesberg, Noupoort, Hanover, Richmond, Beaufort West, Leeu-Gamka, Prince Albert Road and Laingsburg loom on the horizon and disappear behind us one by one. Each one seems to be little more than a cluster of tin-roofed houses and a few shops gathered around the tall spire of the Dutch Reformed Church.

To the passing motorist the Karoo appears to be a great emptiness – endless scrub country punctuated by the occasional windmill and a few black-headed dorper sheep or shaggy white angora goats.

But, to those of us who have lived there, the Karoo is a source of endless fascination and delight.

Here nature has had to adapt to all kinds of extreme conditions. Temperatures rise to over forty degrees Celsius in summer and drop to minus ten and lower in winter. Droughts sometimes last for years, leaving the earth parched and barren; then heavy thunderstorms lash the country and it erupts in a deafening chorus of tiny, clicking frogs. They call and mate and spawn in a frenzy of haste, for who knows when the next rain may fall?

Where have they hidden during all those hot, dusty months?

Farm dams shrink and disappear in the dry years and the clay turns to a hard, cracked crust where animal hooves scratch in vain for a little moisture.

But the first rains soften the earth and allow families of dormant water turtles to emerge, reminding us that this dry land hides a host of hardy creatures far too tough to be destroyed by mere drought and heat.

The plants of the Karoo are small miracles in themselves, capable of incredible feats of rejuvenation. The famous Karoo bush, which sustains great flocks of sheep and goats, might look like burned twigs in the dry times, but even then they provide nourishment all the way down their tough stems, until the animals appear to be chewing the very stones. When the rain comes the Karoo blooms again in a matter of days – some say hours.

The people of this area are no less interesting than the plants and animals.

Like the land itself they may appear dry and tough, but under the hard exterior there's a quiet sense of humour and sly wisdom. There must be if they are to survive the vagaries of this often harsh land.

So, rush across the country to your holiday house in Cape Town if you must. You can pass through this desolate land in a day. Or you can take a little time to stop and listen to its silences, stare in amazement at its miracles and meet some of the people who live and love here.

You might end up richer than before, because not all wealth is measured in money.

FAME AND FACES

I suppose it's natural that a huge area like the Karoo, situated right in the middle of the country, should have its share of famous sons and daughters. And in little Karoo dorps they don't let you forget it.

The Reverend Andrew Murray, who probably did more to spread Christianity in southern Africa than anybody else, left his mark in many a town across the country, starting in Cape Town, where his pale marble statue stands in front of the Groote Kerk, wagging an admonishing finger (now broken) at the naughty world.

(It used to be tradition to place a condom on the great man's finger during the annual University of Cape Town rag float parade. That's no longer possible, which is probably a good thing.)

He is certainly well remembered in Graaff-Reinet, where he once occupied the parsonage. His son, who later became the Rev Charles Murray, laid out the pretty parsonage garden and planted what is now claimed to be the biggest grape vine in the whole world. Anybody who has visited Graaff-Reinet in the heat of mid-summer will understand that the most valued attribute of a grape vine in the Karoo is its shade, not its fruit.

And, talking of grape vines, I have often thought that the Graaff-Reinet vine might be the biggest in the world, but the one on our family farm (appropriately called Grapevale) must certainly be one of the longest.

Many old Karoo farmhouses were designed with a stoep or veranda running right round them to shade the walls.

When my grandfather bought Grapevale in 1923 there were some rather unkempt grape vines in the garden. One of these grew up the pergola over the front entrance of the house, acting as a stoep. As the years passed, the vine, a grape variety called Crystal, was encouraged by careful pruning to grow further and further from its original stem, and today it encircles the whole rambling house with its tendrils, providing welcome shade in summer.

It was always Dad's personal task to prune the vine every winter. When he became too old to clamber up the pruning ladder, he employed one of the farm hands, Banzi Ntame, to do the actual pruning. Dad would sit in a folding chair under the vine and point with his walking stick at the spot where the next cut was to be made. Banzi would lop off the branch and Dad would point at the next spot.

After Dad died Banzi took over the whole job on his own.

By "whole job", I mean he took on both roles.

He set up a folding chair under the vine, sat in it and pointed at the branches overhead with a stick, then climbed up the ladder, cut off the branch and descended to sit in the chair and point at the next spot.

When I asked him why he worked that way he simply said, "That's the way the oubaas and I always used to do it."

You can see the Graaff-Reinet vine in Reinet House, which is the renamed parsonage and a national monument and museum in Murray Street (obviously named after old Andrew). Graaff-Reinet is interesting for a very different reason, too. A few kilometres outside the town, on the road to Middelburg, is a plain white-fronted building where some of the finest tequila in the world is distilled.

We're not allowed to call it tequila, because the Mexicans have grabbed the copyright to the name, but our Agava Gold and Agava Silver have been tasted by the experts and declared every bit as excellent as the best that Mexico can produce.

Tequila is distilled from the fermented juice of the blue agave aloe, known throughout South Africa as the American aloe, or *garingboom*. The spiky plant grows particularly profusely around Graaff-Reinet, which is what prompted the McLaughlin family to establish the distillery there.

Today Graaff-Reinet's tequila is exported to many countries around the world – among them Mexico.

I can't help wondering whether Rev Murray would have approved.

In Beaufort West it's impossible to avoid being told that this is the birthplace of the great heart transplant pioneer, Chris Barnard. They worship the ground he walked on. In fact, they probably have a sample of the ground he walked on in the Chris Barnard Museum in the town's main street.

Visit Steynsburg and you will probably be told that the famous President Paul Kruger was born there. Well, he was born on the farm Bulhoek in the Steynsburg district. Visit the pretty NG Church in Cradock and they will, in all probability, show you that the famous President Paul Kruger's name appears in the church's birth register. Maybe they didn't have a proper birth register in Steynsburg in 1825, or perhaps they felt instinctively that this child was destined for greatness, so it might be a good idea to spread the fame over a wider area.

Middelburg, which is Cradock's next-door neighbour, may not have been the birthplace of statesmen, but it was certainly the original site of General Jan Smuts's farmhouse.

And, when some know-it-all tells you that his farm was situated far away in Irene in Gauteng, tell him he obviously doesn't know the story of the house.

Middelburg was the site of a huge British Army camp during the South African War. After the war – in 1910 – the extensive barracks and other military buildings were handed over to the South African government to be used as an agricultural college. Today Grootfontein Agricultural College is where most of the country's top sheep and wool producers received their training.

At the time of the hand-over there were several prefabricated buildings in the camp that were not needed for the new agricultural college. In due course these came under the auctioneer's hammer and one of them was bought by the future prime minister, Jan Smuts. It was dismantled and transported to his farm Doornkloof, near Irene, where it was re-assembled and is now a national monument. Smuts lived in it until his death in 1950.

CLIMBING THE FAMILY TREE

In the office at our family farm, Grapevale, above the oak roll-top desk is a portrait of a fine-looking old man with a bald head, piercing eyes and large beard. Only the top button of his rough three-piece suit is fastened and a plaited watch chain can be seen tucked into his waistcoat pocket. His fingers are short and stubby, and appear roughened by hard work.

This is Ebenezer Biggs, whom we have always considered to be the father of our large clan. Ebenezer came from a Welsh Quaker family and landed in Algoa Bay (Port Elizabeth) in 1844 aged twenty-four. During the ox-wagon journey to Grahamstown, he was awakened at five o'clock one morning by a strange-looking man. In his letter home to his parents he describes the meeting.

" 'I suppose you do not know me?' said the fellow.

"After looking at him for some time I said, 'No, I do not.'

" 'Your name is Ebenezer, is it not?'

" 'Yes.'

" 'Well, my name is James.'

"Not thinking of meeting my brother, and being still half asleep, I said, 'I do not remember ever having seen you before. What is your name besides James?' When he told me I was quite struck."

Apparently Ebenezer only recognised his brother James when he saw a scar on his forehead that he, Ebenezer, had made when they were children.

In his letter he explains why he hadn't recognised James.

"You will not be surprised I did not know him when I tell you how he was dressed. A blue trouser, yellow waistcoat and white moleskin jacket, and a whip in his hand, but what disguised him most was his aping of the lady by completely covering his straw hat with ostrich feathers, so that I could not see the mark I had made on his forehead. He is about my size, wider across the breast, and an inch shorter." He sounds like quite a character.

James had brought a horse for Ebenezer to ride to Grahamstown where he was "kindly received by the friends" and commenced work the next week "with very pleasant prospects before me".

The next time we pick up Ebenezer's story he was employed as a tutor to the Hobson family at a farm called Harefield near Graaff-Reinet. There he fell in love with one of the Hobson daughters, Mary-Ann, and married her.

Mary-Ann's portrait photograph stares out from the office wall next to that of Ebenezer, a rather stern woman in a high lace collar and black outfit with lace at the cuffs. Her hair is drawn back tightly and she wears a white bonnet.

While she appears fierce at first glance, closer inspection reveals a small twinkle in her eye. Her somewhat pained expression could be there because photographers in those days used slow film and needed to expose it for some time; so they would clamp the heads of their subjects firmly in a sort of neck-brace to prevent any movement.

No doubt I'd have looked a bit unhappy too under the circumstances.

Ebenezer must have met with the Hobson family's approval, because he was given a piece of land called Wellfound, adjoining Harefield, and there he and his bride raised a family of ten children. One of them, George, met a horrible end when he fell into a cauldron of boiling soap at the age of nine. Lily, the youngest daughter, was described as "a delicate girl and died quite young".

My father wrote of the family: "These Biggs sons of Ebenezer were all farmers. They acquired good farms, developed them and lived their lives on their farms with no

other interests except improving the land and living in peace and harmony with everyone – lovers of the land, sound stock farmers, good family people and very community conscious."

(While he may not have realised it, Dad was describing himself exactly.)

Clement, one of the sons, married Mabel Winifred Collett in 1902 and moved away to the Steynsburg district, where he bought a farm that he named Glenelg, after a place he had visited while on a study trip to the Quakers of New Zealand. He liked the sound of the name and also the fact that it could be spelled forwards or backwards. Clement and Winifred raised six children, two sons and four daughters, on Glenelg and then moved to the family's present farm, Grapevale, in the Colesberg district in 1920.

One of the sons, Llewellyn, moved to Wellfound, married another Hobson, Florence, known in the family as "Fotty", and had three children, one of whom is running Wellfound today.

The other son, Norman, stayed at Grapevale, married Clarice Rogers, a farmer's daughter from Middelburg, and had three children, two sons and a daughter. Norman's younger son, Roger, now runs the farm.

By the time Roger took over the running of Grapevale it had been developed into one of the finest farms in the district. The veld had been well cared for and the stock, after many years of careful selection, was in magnificent condition.

The Biggs family doesn't go in for elaborate tombstones or memorials.

When Norman died the family erected a small brass plaque on the pillar of the front gate. It bears the short inscription: "Grapevale is his memorial."

COLLETT CONNECTION

There is an old Karoo saying: "If you kick a bush in the Eastern Cape a Collett will probably pop out." Almost any story of the Eastern Cape (much of which falls into the area known as the Karoo) will sooner or later include a Collett.

The Colletts are a large, rambling family, whose meandering bloodlines are interwoven with those of the Biggses, the Trollips and the Butlers. Tradition has it that the first Collett to arrive in South Africa, James Lydford Collett, landed in Cape Town in about 1823 on a ship bound for Bombay. He was working his passage as tutor to the family of a returning Indian Army officer.

Apparently he had left England in something of a hurry after a rather nasty incident involving sleepwalking. The family tended to gloss over the details. In Cape Town he either jumped ship or failed to get back to the harbour in time to catch the boat when it sailed (depending on who's telling the story), and was stranded with only the clothes he wore and no money at all. No innkeeper would offer him lodgings, as he was penniless, so he wandered about in the gathering dusk and eventually crept into a still-warm Dutch oven, where he spent his first night in Africa.

Professor Guy Butler, in his autobiography *Karoo Morning*, says that some of the more haughty members of the Collett family have always fiercely denied this story.

Gervase, one of James's grandsons, is reported to have said, "My grandfather never slept in any oven, least of all a Dutchman's."

Whatever his beginnings in this country, old James seems to have prospered as a trader and farmer and was elected to the Cape parliament in 1854.

Granny Biggs (Mabel Winifred, known in the district as Aunt Winnie) was a Collett and always seemed to be collecting distant Collett relatives who needed shelter from life's storms, and bringing them to the farm to stay – sometimes for years and years. Her husband, Clement Biggs, accepted these invasions of their home with resignation and patience. I remember one such visitor particularly well.

A traveller passing through the district heard that Gran was a Collett and said, "Collett? There's an old Mr Collett who is the barman at the hotel in Daniëlskuil. I wonder if he is any relation of yours."

Gran asked what his first name was and heard that it was Arthur.

"That's my brother," she said, and promptly wrote to him, inviting him to stay at Grapevale.

Gran and Uncle Arthur came from a very large family (they would later spend endless hours arguing about which brothers and sisters were older or younger). When Arthur was a teenager it became increasingly obvious that the family farm could not provide a living for all the Collett boys, so he bid the family farewell and set off to seek his fortune at the age of sixteen.

The story goes that his parting words were, "I'll either come home when I am rich, or not at all. Goodbye."

And none of the family heard from him again. He was in his late seventies when Gran learned of his whereabouts in Daniëlskuil.

In the intervening years Arthur had lived a life of high adventure, working wherever he could to raise money to mount yet another hunting expedition into the interior. He would travel by ox wagon, living by hunting until his money was exhausted, then sell his team and wagon and find work wherever he was, to raise money for his next adventure. His jobs included being a barber and a blacksmith on the railway project building the line to Delagoa Bay.

"I used to sharpen picks for the labourers," he told me. "I set up my forge at the side of the line and they'd bring me the picks when the points had worn away."

On one occasion when he was a transport driver taking a family of Americans from Port Elizabeth to Delagoa Bay (now Maputo) he came across thousands of people digging and pegging out claims "in the veld near Pretoria", as he described it. One of his friends urged him to stay and stake a claim, as gold had been discovered.

He promised he'd do so when he returned. And, by the time he made his way back to the place, it was the bustling mining city of Johannesburg.

"Who knows?" he used to say. "I might have ended up owning a farm in Eloff Street if I'd stopped there."

In his wanderings, he learned a great deal about the whole of southern Africa and was pounced upon eagerly by Paul Kruger's commandos during the South African War and conscripted as a scout.

"They gave me the choice of joining them or being shot, because I was English speaking," he said. "I thought it would be best for me if I joined them."

Later he was captured by the British troops, who valued his linguistic talents and signed him up as an interpreter when they interrogated Boer prisoners.

So he ended up serving both sides in turn and later managed to wangle not one, but two ex-serviceman's pensions. Admittedly they were not particularly generous pensions.

Uncle Arthur's memory remained pin-sharp until his death, but his hearing began to fail much earlier. He would sit in his favourite chair on Gran's veranda, oblivious to the conversation around him, then suddenly boom out in his very penetrating voice: "It was on September the twelfth, which was a Thursday – no, it was a Friday – and we were laying over near Barberton with General Steyn's commando when we heard news of a British force heading our way..." And all conversation would die as the story unfolded in minute detail. I've often wished I had had a tape recorder in those days. What a history I could have collected.

Another faculty that remained very much alive was his speed of hand. A fly would settle on his left arm and in a flash his right hand would move to slap it to death. He never missed. We youngsters used to try the fly-slapping trick endlessly, but never got it right. Karoo flies are no slouches.

Arthur never married, but had apparently been something of a ladies' man in his more sprightly days. He once told me the naughty story of an adventure in Durban, where he was courting a beautiful young lady.

He decided to take her home in a rickshaw after dining and wining her, and as they settled into the vehicle he said to the rickshaw man, in Zulu, which he spoke well, "Take a long route to this lady's house, and go slowly, because I want to make love to her on the way."

The journey proceeded successfully and when he dropped his partner off at her home, much, much later, she gave him a goodnight kiss and thanked him for a wonderful evening.

In perfect Zulu.

When he came to stay with us, Uncle Arthur had few needs, but he did enjoy his brandy. Most of his pension went straight to his sister to pay for his board, but enough was kept out to pay for a case of a dozen bottles of Mellowwood brandy every week. The post bus would call every Tuesday and Friday, and Tuesday's bus was Arthur's brandy delivery.

By then his supply would be depleted and he would glance anxiously down the road every few minutes until the bus arrived. The case would be stowed in his room and peace would reign again.

I never saw him drunk, or even mildly tipsy, but he would excuse himself from the company from time to time and disappear down the passage, to reappear a few minutes later, wiping his mouth with a handkerchief, ready to regale us with yet another story of his escapades, or one of the songs the British troops used to sing on long marches.

The Colletts are known for their longevity, and Gran and Uncle Arthur eventually moved to a small cottage in Port Alfred, where they spent their remaining years surrounded by nieces and nephews. Uncle Arthur died at the age of ninety-nine. Gran lived alone for some years and every now and then the family would receive news that she had been taken seriously ill. So the clan would head for Port Alfred to pay their last respects.

And she'd open her eyes, see us standing round her bed and say, "Ah, we have enough to make up a foursome. Somebody get the cards while I get up."

Bridge was one of her passions.

There were four or five of these false alarms.

Eventually, when I was living in Bloemfontein, I received the news that Gran had passed away. Immediately I set off to be with the family in Port Alfred. My first stop was to be at the farm in Colesberg and I arrived there just before midnight and drove straight up to the staff houses. One by one the farm labourers emerged, blinking and yawning, to see what was happening.

There, under a full moon, I gave them the news that the Oumies had died and I was on my way to the funeral.

Immediately Ndoyisile Maliti, known as Longlegs, said he would accompany me and we set off at dawn for Port Alfred. All the way down he told me stories of the old lady's life and of the many people who had worked for her.

I had my own memories of her, and in all of them she was active and busy. She knitted untiringly, she bottled fruit, made butter, brewed delicious ginger beer with the corks firmly tied down with string. Even when she relaxed in her favourite chair on her veranda, her hands would be busy shelling peas, stringing beans or cutting up fruit for a fruit salad.

After the burial service, when the mourners had departed, Ndoyisile stood alone and silent for a long while at the graveside, then took a handful of earth and tossed it onto the coffin.

"She was a good person," he said quietly.

I think she was.

INTERNET ANCESTOR

Few people living in today's world of instant communications can appreciate the impact of the first telephone lines to the remote areas of the Karoo.

Until the advent of the telephone, all communication travelled at the speed of the horse. If you wished to get a message to your neighbour, you sent a horseman across the veld to deliver it. When you needed a doctor, you would set off for the nearest town on horseback, riding as fast as you could to the next farm, where you'd be given a fresh horse to take you to the following farm. With luck and hard riding you might reach the doctor in time to save the patient.

In the early 1900s nine farmers in the Noupoort district decided to pool their resources and erect a telephone line to the town. This was no small undertaking. They called in the assistance of a Mr Watson, a former post office employee with some knowledge of erecting telephone lines. He was given the task of finding and buying the necessary material for the new line. It would require forty kilometres of double bronze wire, and enough poles to stretch over the mountains to the town, where it would end at Mr Wilmot's general dealer's store.

. Mr Watson found and bought a large number of discarded steel boiler tubes from the railways to act as telephone poles and slowly, one by one, the poles were set up along the winding dirt road. Mr Watson supervised the work and the hard labour was supplied by farm labourers from the nine farms.

They managed to find enough discarded telephones, made by the Swedish company Ericsson and no longer required by the post office. They were large wooden-cased machines with a speaking trumpet fixed to the front (adjustable for height) and an earpiece attached by a separate cord. On the side was a winder, which operated a generator to produce the electricity necessary to make the phone ring. Eventually the "Number One Line" was ready for use. Life changed dramatically from that moment. Suddenly, instead of taking weeks, a message could be sent from a remote farmhouse to anywhere in the world in a matter of hours. The farmer would simply telephone Mr Wilmot and dictate his message. This would be jotted down, probably on the side of a brown paper bag, and taken across the road to the post office where it was sent as a telegram (in Morse code) to anywhere in the world. News of Granny's death or the birth of Lucy's latest baby could be flashed to Cape Town or even London in less than a day.

E-mail, cell-phones and the Internet are mere refinements of this one giant step for human communication. You can see the very first private telephone ever used in South Africa in Matjiesfontein's fascinating museum. It was installed by James Logan, founder of the village, to link his farm, Tweedside, to the town.

For many years my father, who was a young learner farmer, was the official linesman for the Number One Line. Whenever there was a fault, he would gather up his tools and set off on horseback to find and repair it. A common problem in winter was ice that formed on the wires, causing them to sag ever lower until they snapped. Dad would have to climb each pole adjacent to the break, undo the wires from their insulators and lay them on the icy ground. Then he would find a handy dry cowpat and make a fire to heat his soldering iron, so he could repair the break. He discovered that the stirrup from his saddle could be attached to the top of the telephone pole to provide a footrest while he reattached the wires. Without this handy step it was almost impossible to keep a grip on the icy pole.

The Number One Line was a typical country "party line". Each subscriber had a call signal. Ours was three long rings (number 103) while our nearest neighbour's was two short rings (number 120). Of course anybody could listen in to all the conversations, although nobody ever admitted to doing this. We knew some of the less busy wives made it their business to monitor all the telephone traffic.

In one oft-repeated tale, two women were chatting when they heard the tiny click of a third telephone being picked up. They suspected that Tannie Sarah was listening, so they steered the conversation to some rather controversial topic and, after some argument this way and that, one of them said, "Isn't that so, Tannie Sarah?" And, without thinking, Tannie Sarah answered, "Yes, it is," and then slammed down her receiver in embarrassment. She didn't show her face in public for a few weeks after that.

Proper telephone etiquette required you to lift the handset and ask, "Is the line clear?" If there was no reply, you could start your call by cranking the handle at the side of the machine to send the code ring – three longs, two shorts, or a short and two longs, as the case may be. At the end of the call you gave one short ring to signal to other users that the line was now clear again.

In time all the subscribers got to know each other's ringing style. "Oh, that's Oom Jan calling Uncle Ivan, but he's in Middelburg." And you'd lift your phone and say, "Oom Jan, Uncle Ivan isn't home. You should try him later this evening."

Of course, once the line had been incorporated into the general system, all calls to numbers not on the same party line had to be routed through the telephone exchange in Noupoort. It was a warm and personal system. Quite often I'd call my parents from Cape Town, only to be told, "One-oh-three are not at home this evening. They're visiting seven-four-oh. I'll put you through to them."

Who needed answering machines?

Those first party line telephones were far more than mere communication. They were a source of endless entertainment. I heard of a very musical family, the Vorsters, who lived on the farm Berenskraal in the Middelburg district and used their phone to share their talent with the neighbours. From time to time they would call up the others on their line and announce: "We're singing tonight, in case you'd like to listen." Then they'd leave their telephone handset dangling from the machine and pump up the old harmonium to accompany the family choir. All the other subscribers on the line would sit there with their receivers pressed to their ears, enjoying the informal Vorster concert.

Today's automatic dialling system may be faster and more efficient, but it certainly lacks the personal touch of the old party line and exchange operator.

Footnote

Some years after the erection of the Number One Line, the Post Office began installing telephone lines in all country areas. The Number One Line was incorporated into the system and stayed in operation for a further fifteen years, with the subscribers paying a far lower rental fee than the rest of the district's telephone users. When the telephones lines were eventually standardised, a completely new line was erected and the old line dismantled. The material from the Number One Line was divided among the original members and most of it ended up as fencing material.

The Roar of the Open Road

In the Karoo, probably more than in most other places, one realises just how fast life has changed in the last century or so.

People tend to live a long time in the clean, dry air of the Karoo and there are still many old folks around who can recall the first person in the district to own a car, or to have a telephone installed in their home.

My father, for one, had a very clear memory of the first time a car drove past their farm, Glenelg, in the Steynsburg district.

"We had heard about this amazing cart that didn't need horses to pull it," he told me, "but we only half believed it. Then one day we children were playing on the koppie behind the house, armed with wooden sticks and attacking an enemy army of prickly pear bushes, when we heard this strange roaring sound coming from the road.

"And there in the distance, kicking up a huge cloud of dust, was one of those horseless carts. We all dropped our weapons and raced down to the road to get a closer look. It came roaring past at a fearful speed and we ventured cautiously into the road when it had passed.

"We had been told that these things produced a strange smell from their behinds, so we all knelt down in the dust and sniffed the road. Indeed, there was a strange unfamiliar smell there."

Thus did the age of motoring arrive in the back-roads of the Karoo.

Much later, when I became aware of motoring and cars, all the country roads had gates across them. The sixty-kilometre stretch of road from our farm to Middelburg had no fewer than thirteen gates on it.

At each gate the car had to stop, somebody had to get out and open the gate; the driver then drove through and waited while the gate was closed and the passenger returned to his or her seat.

It was a tedious business.

Fortunately many of the gates were close to farmsteads and there were often small children playing nearby who were ready to run down and open the gate in exchange for a handful of sweets or a small coin.

Every motorist made sure there was a packet of rewards on board for the gate-openers. It was well worth the small expense and provided the farm kids with rare treats. Shopkeepers in country towns knew exactly what you meant if you asked for a packet of "gate-opener sweets".

Some of the more daring and reckless young motorists learned that they could drive up close to a gate and nudge it open with the bumper of the car. Cars came with sturdy steel bumpers in those days. Gate catches were rather flimsy affairs, usually made of a hook of number 8 fencing wire.

Of course this manoeuvre meant the gate was left open after the car had passed and was frowned upon by farmers. Soon they developed a diabolical device to foil the gatecrashers – the split gate.

This consisted of a gate divided horizontally, with the bottom half loosely attached to the top, which was connected to the gate catch. Should any naughty motorist decide to push it open instead of opening it the legal way, the bottom half of the gate would obligingly swing open, leaving the top half still closed and at exactly the right height to smash the car's windscreen.

Fortunately cattle grids were introduced before the wicked split gates became too widespread, or they might have led to war among neighbours.

Today most public country roads are securely fenced on both sides to prevent animals wandering onto the road. It's a serious offence to have untended stock on a public road. In most districts the gates and grids have long gone and the drive to Middelburg can now be accomplished without a stop.

I was surprised recently to encounter several cattle grids on the winding, dusty road from Laingsburg through the area known as the "Moordenaarskaroo" (Murderers' Karoo) to Sutherland. I hadn't seen a cattle grid for many years and they brought back quite fond memories of those childhood trips to Middelburg.

THE REAL PIONEERS

In almost every little Karoo town you'll find a synagogue, usually now used as something else – a museum, perhaps, or a library or possibly a private home.

The story behind these buildings is similar in every Karoo dorp. Only the names are different.

One of the features of early Karoo country life was the Jewish *"smous"* (peddler). (My late grandmother always pronounced the word to rhyme with "house".) These hardy and determined men were usually immigrants whose families had fled the pogroms of Eastern Europe and arrived, penniless, to start a new life in the young South Africa. They were used to hardship and poverty. They knew about barter and trade.

Somehow they gathered a pack of small, portable items to sell, often assisted by immigrants who had arrived before them. With their heavy packs of goods on their backs, they would set off on foot across the great empty plains in search of customers. They knew their best bet was to get as far as possible from the towns where the goods they were selling were readily available.

Karoo farms were far apart and their inhabitants had very little opportunity to shop. The arrival of the *smous* was an important event in the life of the farm family. Mother could buy the sewing thread and buttons she needed to repair her husband's clothes. A yard of tough khaki material would be useful for patching his work trousers. There might even be a few pennies over to spend on luxuries like lace for a collar or ribbon for a blouse to wear to *nagmaal* in the town.

If he was lucky, the *smous* would be offered a hot meal before he set off again. Sometimes not.

By sheer hard work the peddler eventually saved enough to buy a packhorse or mule, and could double the amount of stock he could carry. Later he might get a cart to take him on his rounds. One day he would find himself with enough money saved to set up a shop in the nearest town, settle down, find a wife and raise a family.

Every Karoo town had its Jewish shopkeepers and hoteliers: the Seligmans, the Musikanths, the Lustons and the Shapiros.

Following Jewish tradition they valued education above all else and made sure their children would not have to struggle through life as they had. Sons and daughters were sent to good schools and universities. They became doctors, lawyers, engineers and businessmen in the big cities.

When their parents retired they moved to the cities too, to be near their successful children. Slowly the Jewish communities dwindled in each little Karoo town until there were only nine families left.

In order to have an official Jewish congregation there must be ten heads of family forming the *minyan*, or quorum. With only nine the synagogue could no longer function. It was sold and the remaining families moved away.

When you're travelling through the Karoo, take time to find the old *schul* in each Karoo town. Stand and wonder at the story behind it.

Many of the country's successful Jewish families now established in Johannesburg, Cape Town and Durban have their South African roots deep in the dusty soil of the Karoo.

Hantams, New and Old

For as long as anybody can remember the part of the Karoo where I grew up has been knows as the "Hantam".

Each Saturday the neighbours gather at the tennis club on our farm, where the fading painted sign proclaims it to be the "Hantam Tennis Club".

Church services are held there whenever a minister visits the area. It makes little difference whether the cleric is an Anglican, a Methodist or any other denomination. Everybody rolls up, gives generously to the collection plate and enjoys sociable tea and cakes afterwards.

Many of the Hantam couples were married in the Tennis Club, and every summer school holidays there are dances and parties in the clubhouse.

Saturdays see a gathering of farmers, their families and any visitors who might be around, for "tennis". This usually consists of one or two leisurely sets of tennis, played before a hugely critical group of idle spectators who claim to be too old or too tired actually to play, but who are always willing to offer loud advice and criticism.

"What's the matter, Peter? Locusts ate a hole in your racquet?"

At one time the Hantam tennis team was one of the strongest in the local league and competed successfully against teams like the Tafelberg team from the Middelburg area, and the Schoombee team, for an imaginary trophy known as the "Mossie Cup".

Recently some of the Hantam families have left the area and the children have grown up and migrated to the cities, and as a result the local population has changed in character.

Today there are a few stalwarts who turn up every Saturday and actually play tennis, and several others, like myself, who arrive at the clubhouse when the sun is low on the horizon and wait for the club bar to open.

There are three splendid concrete tennis courts at the club, but these days there are seldom more than two in use.

Some visitors are confused about the name "Hantam". They point out that the "real" Hantam is far away in the Calvinia district.

This is true.

I believe the word "hantam" was the old Khoi name for a particular species of indigenous bush that grows on the slopes of the mountains now known as the Hantamberge, near Calvinia.

Long ago farmers from the Hantam area moved away, looking for better farming areas, and discovered a promising region to the south of Colesberg, which reminded them of their old Hantam. They named it *De Nuwe Hantam* (The New Hantam) and applied for the right to farm there.

All the land in this area was state owned at that time and farmers were granted portions on a leasehold basis. They paid what was known as an annual "quit rent" for the use of the land. This situation remained in place until about the time when Sir Benjamin d'Urban was governor of the Cape (from 1834).

By this time Colesberg had been declared an official magisterial district and the land around the town was divided into wards. Our part was known as "Ward Hantam".

Some of the families who had settled on the quit rent farms wanted to own their properties, so that they could leave them to their heirs when they died, and applied for freehold rights. When this was granted the farmers no longer paid quit rents but had to fork out property rates instead.

You get nothing for nothing, but at least the land was theirs to develop and hand over in good condition to their children and grandchildren.

On many of the older deeds of transfer one still sees the phrase: "A certain piece of Quit Rent free land, known as..." Several title deeds describe the farms as "Malan's Request" or "Herbert's Request", indicating that the request had been submitted for ownership when the original deed was drawn up.

Eventually, of course, the whole of the Hantam area became privately owned and several of the farms have been in the possession of the same families for considerably longer than a century.

Strangely enough, there's a strong link between the Hantam (our Hantam) and Boschendal, the famous wine and fruit estate in the Franschhoek area.

In about 1900 a syndicate was formed by three of the country's richest financiers – Cecil John Rhodes, Sir Abe Bailey and Alfred Beit – with the object of acquiring farming land throughout the country. Boschendal was one of the properties they owned, and in the Colesberg district the RBB Syndicate ended up owning forty properties on which sheep and other livestock were farmed.

Having access to a great deal of money, the syndicate set about developing their properties. They erected good fences, drilled boreholes and set up windmills for watering the animals. They built several dams for irrigation purposes and generally improved the farms. The farm Grootfontein became the headquarters of Sir Abe Bailey, who was the most actively involved of the partners. He established an elegant homestead with formal gardens and well-planned outbuildings, all of which are still in use today.

Farm managers were installed on most of the farms, and Mr Morton Barnes-Webb was appointed the general manager of the whole project, with his headquarters on Oorlogspoort, which became the focal point of the syndicate's activities. (His grandson, Peter Barnes-Webb, is a successful farmer in the district and today manages the original Bailey home farm, Grootfontein.) This injection of capital did a great deal to speed up the development of the area far faster than would have been possible if left to individual farmers. Two large dams were built by the syndicate during 1909 and 1910 – one on the farm Macasserfontein and the other on Grapevale, which is our family's home farm today.

The Grapevale Dam was built across the Oorlogspruit River, which eventually finds its way into the Gariep (Orange) River and was made – as were most dams in those days – of earth scooped out from what was to be the inside of the dam, using small earth scoops drawn by teams of oxen. My father told me that at the height of building operations more than a hundred oxen were in action at any one time. He also said that about a hundred oxen died on the job during the operation.

The dam had hardly been finished when it filled up and overflowed, creating an impressive man-made (or ox-made) lake. The depth of water near the bank was about eight metres and the bank was two hundred and fifty metres long. The water stood back some seven hundred metres from the bank.

Below this impressive dam, seventy hectares of lands were cultivated for the growing of crops like wheat and lucerne. Fish were introduced and angling became a popular pastime, particularly among the local coloured community. Canoeing and swimming were regular weekend activities.

Grapevale's dam provided irrigation water for half a century, but the annual influx of silt made it progressively shallower. In 1960 it dried up completely for the first time, leaving thousands of dead fish on the muddy bottom. Since then it has dried up several times and is no longer used for irrigation purposes.

During one of its dry periods I decided to use it as a runway for a small two-seater aircraft I owned and kept in Bloemfontein, where I was living at the time. After completing several successful landings and take-offs I became overly bold and forgot to check the wind direction before coming in to land.

The little plane floated on and on a few centimetres above the earth, stubbornly refusing to settle down, and ended up crashing dramatically into the long reeds at the far end, where it slowly flipped over onto its back, leaving my sister-in-law, Penny, and me hanging upside down by our seat-belts in a most undignified fashion. We crawled out no worse for the incident apart from my seriously injured dignity and damaged reputation as a pilot.

The dam at Macasserfontein is still in use, but has a small catchment area and seldom fills, although it does not suffer the same silt problem that faced Grapevale's dam.

As the RBB Syndicate bought more and more properties, some of the long established families in the area became alarmed that all the farms in the district would eventually be incorporated into the big farming empire. They protected their properties by having them entailed for a specified number of generations. This meant the farm could not be sold, but had to go to the oldest son of each successive generation.

This left pockets of privately owned land dotted throughout the syndicate land, and several of these entailed properties are still occupied by descendants of the original owners today.

The RBB Syndicate eventually decided to sell the Colesberg farms and they were offered for sale, one by one. Today only four farms are still owned by descendants of the late Sir Abe Bailey. One of these owners, Will Bailey, is a regular member of the Hantam tennis club, but like mine his tennis revolves more around the bar than the court.

As Milton might have said: "They also serve, who only sit and wait for opening time."

Mermaids and Cowboys

When the shadows of the poplar trees grow long over the tennis court at the Hantam Tennis Club, the old folks on the clubhouse stoep lose interest in the last set and start casting worried glances inside and asking each other whether it isn't later than usual for the secretary to open the bar. They could have sworn they heard the Boeing pass overhead quite a while back.

And the secretary apologises and says he thought Johannes had the keys to the bar, but Johannes is still on the court, so they send one of his sons to get them from him, and he says he doesn't have them, but he saw them hanging on a hook in the kitchen next to the bar door. And after some flurried activity everybody has a glass in their hand and the conversation becomes more animated.

"Did they ever find out about that mermaid that was supposed to be seen at Meiringspoort?"

"Ag, rubbish, man."

"No, seriously. Apparently people have seen a sort of mermaid creature down there among the deep kloofs of the poort, where there are some rock pools that hardly ever get the sun on them. There was a newspaper story not long ago that the floods had washed the mermaid out and it landed up dead on the beach at Mossel Bay. They say there are old Khoi rock paintings there in the poort and you can clearly see a figure with the top half of a human and a sort of fish body from the waist down."

"Ja, boet, you hear some funny stories in the Karoo."

Of course everybody knows the story about the hitchhiking ghost of the Karoo. It must be true because one of the club members has a sister whose husband was driving along the N1 one misty night when he saw this young girl hitching at the side of the road. He stopped and she climbed in and they chatted for a while; then she went silent and he looked round to see whether she had fallen asleep or what... and there was nobody there.

Man, did he get a shock!

He pulled into the hotel at Leeu-Gamka and ordered a stiff double brandy and Coke and told the barman what had happened.

And the barman said, yes, it wasn't the first time. He'd heard the same story from quite a few people.

Apparently there was a young girl who was killed in an accident at that exact spot some years ago, when she was on the pillion of her boyfriend's motorbike. And they say her ghost has been trying to hitch a lift home ever since.

I've never seen the Khoi rock painting of the mermaid and, although I have travelled the N1 for many years, no pretty hitchhiker has needed a lift from me.

Still, that doesn't mean the stories aren't true.

Some of the mysterious characters in Karoo stories probably have more substance than the mermaids and misty motorcycle maidens.

There's the notorious Texas Jack, for example.

Pam Avis (née Collett), eighty-four, told of her encounter with Texas Jack in a story she shared with readers of *Rose's Roundup*, a regular newsletter distributed by Rose Willis from Beaufort West.

"It was a scorching hot Karoo day in 1926," Pam said. "My sisters and I were playing on the shady veranda of our lovely old farmhouse on De Keur, the family farm near Middelburg. Suddenly the clip-clop of hooves, jangle of metal pots and pans and rattle of wheels interrupted our game.

"A brightly painted wagon drawn by two sweating mules slowly emerged from the dust of the rocky road leading to our house. As it clanked to a stop a rangy man, dressed in a checked shirt, huge Stetson and high boots, stepped down. He was the most unusual creature we'd ever seen. As my dad, Gervase Collett, went to greet him, the man said, 'Good day, I'm Texas Jack. Would you like a magic show?'

"What a question! We all quickly settled on the veranda to watch."

Texas Jack then put on a magnificent show with magic rings, cards, ropes and sleight of hand tricks.

"He was fantastic. Texas Jack asked for Gervase's pocket watch. With some trepidation Dad handed over his precious timepiece. Texas Jack tossed it into a bag, which he smashed about on the table. We were horrified. Dad nearly had a fit. Then Texas Jack produced the watch intact from the back of Dad's jacket amid sighs of relief all round!"

Gervase Collett was a kindly man and offered Texas Jack a night's rest in a vacant overseer's cottage. This was gratefully accepted. The mules were set to graze. Milk, meat and eggs were sent from the farmhouse and soon everyone settled down for the night. Early next morning Gervase popped down to see whether Texas Jack had spent a restful night.

"Dad came stomping back in a rage," Pam recalls. "Not only had Texas Jack decamped during the night, but he had also helped himself to a number of things from the cottage."

No doubt many other Karoo farmers in the area enjoyed the wonders of Texas Jack's disappearing trick before he set off to seek new audiences in regions where his fame had not yet spread.

And, after all, the loss of a few possessions from a foreman's cottage is a small price to pay for a good story that has entertained friends for three generations.

Texas Jack, it seems, was more than just a wandering con man.

Just after the South African War he appeared on the scene with a host of Wild West characters calling themselves Texas Jack's Wild West Show.

The following story also comes from *Rose's Roundup*.

According to an article written by Professor Guy Butler, Texas Jack used to boast that he or one of his riders could stick to the back of any bronco from any place in the world. Their boast went one step further: they'd lasso any piece of wild horseflesh from anywhere and ride it.

The men from the Quaggashoek mountain area near Cradock invited Texas Jack to come and see some "horseflesh" that they bet he would never ride. They took him into the mountains and showed him the mountain zebras. Texas Jack accepted their bet: one hundred pounds (big money in those days).

A date was set for the challenge.

Texas Jack and his men set up a huge public picnic. Ringside seats were sold. Deckchairs were set out on the hillside. Binoculars, coffee, rusks, biltong and glasses of alcohol were supplied. A great crowd gathered. Excitement filled the air. The cowboys, true entertainers, rode into the valley in a posse. They waved. The crowd cheered. Texas Jack's plan was bold and simple. It was based on the Red Indian method of hunting buffalo: exhaust the zebras before trying to lasso and mount them. It worked. He and his cowboys drove the animals up and down the valley several times. Eventually, when they were exhausted, Texas Jack roped one and mounted it. The zebra was too tired to buck.

The crowd straggled off, greatly disappointed. This was not the show they'd expected. Yet the farmers paid up.

A Karoo farmer is not the sort of man to renege on a gambling debt.

NEVER-ENDING STORY

Time passes at a leisurely pace in the Karoo and there's always time for a story. Some stories take longer to tell than others.

Shearing time is a busy time on the farm.

In the hot tin-roofed shearing shed the gangs of shearers stand hunched over their sheep, their shears clicking away as the white fleeces are rolled back from the submissive sheep.

As each sheep is finished the shearer stands up, straightens his tired back and lets the sheep go back to the flock before catching the next one.

The fleece-thrower gathers up the wool skilfully into a bundle, takes it to the sorting table and floats it out to land in a flat carpet in front of the sorters.

The sorters – usually the farmer himself and one or two of his most skilled workers – trim off the side pieces that are tangled with thorns, toss away the dirty bits of scruffy wool, strip out the back wool where the dust of a year has settled, and decide on the grade of the best wool that remains. Wool is sorted by fineness and length.

The trimmings are tossed to the "piece-pickers" at the next table for the next step in the sorting process.

It's repetitive work and the long day is punctuated by scraps of conversation, quiet jokes, and stories about neighbours and friends and family members who have left to find work in the cities.

"What ever happened to young Dumpie?" my brother, Roger, asked at the sorting table one day. Dumpie – never known for his intelligence or skills – had left the farm some time ago.

"Dumpie?" said Nzame Maliti, sorting alongside. "He's done very well for himself. When he left here he went and got his heavy-duty licence, and now he drives a big lorry for the railways. He makes a lot of money and has bought a house in Noupoort."

"I can't believe it," said Roger. "Dumpie was always too stupid to do anything right. Well, well, imagine him being a successful lorry driver!" And the conversation drifted to something else as the long day slipped by.

A year later, when the shears were clicking again and the sorters stood at the table picking out the grades of wool, Roger mentioned casually that he was still interested that old Dumpie had done so well.

"Oh, you should just see him now!" said Nzame. "He bought his own lorry and is in business for himself. In fact, he has two lorries and pays somebody to drive the other one. He moved into one of the biggest houses in Noupoort."

Again this news was greeted with amazement. Just imagine! Stupid old Dumpie who always seemed too dumb to handle a wheelbarrow, much less a heavy lorry. Who would have thought it?

Another year rolled by.

Back at the sorting table, Roger happened to mention the miracle of Dumpie who had achieved so much.

"Dumpie?" said Nzame. "What has he ever achieved?"

"Well, you said last year that he owned two lorries and a big house in Noupoort," said Roger.

"Dumpie?" laughed Nzame. "His own house? He's too stupid to own even a pondok in the squatter camp. He works as a labourer down at Van Wyk's farm. He's still just as useless as he ever was."

After a stunned silence, Roger stuttered, "But you said..."

"Ag yes, I know," said Nzame casually, trimming off the side of a fleece, "but that was just a story to help pass the day away."

And the real story that everybody chuckles about today is how Nzame managed to spin out a completely fictitious tale over three shearing seasons.

That takes real story-telling skill.

Under the Spreading Chestnut Tree

As is the case all over the world, the Karoo village blacksmith was always an important part of farm life. The blacksmith's shop was a dark, mysterious place where men gathered round the anvil and a great wheezing forge heated metal horseshoes and wheel rims to glowing red. Heavy sledge hammers clanged down on hot steel, sparks flew in showers and thick metal flowed into new shapes.

A good blacksmith could shape the heavy drawbar for a two-furrow plough, or form hot steel into the most delicate spirals and curved leaf designs for a garden gate. The blacksmith was a true artist.

Things have changed in recent years and if you want steel heated you're more likely to use an oxy-acetylene torch than a blacksmith's forge.

But people have not changed as much as we like to think and most Karoo towns still have the modern equivalent of the village blacksmith's shop. Often it is a yard with no sign outside to indicate its purpose, but farmers all know this is where they bring a broken gate hinge to be welded, or a bent harrow tine to be straightened, or a tractor drawbar to be re-shaped. Here you'll find the man who mends machines – really mends them instead of merely ordering a replacement part from the agent, at vast cost and waste of time.

In Colesberg Piet Vorster is the nearest you could get to a village blacksmith. Apart from owning an incredible collection of scrap, Piet is the expert windmill repairer of the area. If he can't find a replacement part among the heaps of assorted scrap in his yard, he will make one for you. Just leave it there in the corner and he will get to it when he has a chance. The yard is cluttered with – well – stuff of every description and some far beyond description. Old ploughs lean against piles of fencing wire, and chicken coops vie for space with discarded beds and black coal stoves, while chipped white washing machines and motorcycle parts are tangled together with ornate brass gaslight fittings from a bygone age in what looks like a complex modern sculpture.

And in the far corner, faded but still a noble sight, is a complete stagecoach. It once probably carried the mail and passengers on a regular route from Colesberg to Bloemfontein, or maybe Kimberley. It must have covered many thousands of miles in its day. Now it stands wedged between farm implements and broken furniture. Its leather seats are cracked and it could do with several coats of new varnish and some tightening up of steel wheel tyres.

Piet loves his things and is always reluctant to part with anything he has accumulated. One day a farmer delivered a windmill head with a cracked sump and, after they'd discussed the repair, the talk, as ever, turned to life in general and the strangeness of people in particular.

"Ja, Meneer," said Piet, "people can be very odd. Do you know, the other day a chap from Bloemfontein walked in here and offered me fifty thousand rands for that post coach."

"Fifty thousand rands!" said the impressed farmer. "Hell Piet, that's a lot of money. When is he coming to collect it?"

"What?" said Piet indignantly. "You think I'd sell that coach?"

"But fifty thousand rands is a good price, man."

"Ja, that may be, but what the hell would I do without a post coach?"

People can indeed be strange.

It's not easy to find a proper blacksmith's shop today, but the tradition is kept alive here and there.

There's a restored blacksmith's workshop in the Kleinplasie open-air farm museum in Worcester and another on the rebuilt Crafts Green in Swellendam. Both are used from time to time for displays of the way things used to be done.

Here, in scenes that must have been similar centuries ago, small groups of boys gather round in the dusty smithy to gape in awe as the heavy hammer clangs down on white-hot steel, sending the sparks dancing, and a newly sharpened pick-head plunges hissing into a tub of water to temper the fire-formed steel.

One hopes the tradition will be continued, but there are not many craftsmen left today who understand the mysteries of the forge and anvil.

OSTRICHES AND OPTIMISM

Sooner or later, it seems, every Karoo farmer decides to try ostrich farming.

Just look at the benefits. Ostriches are indigenous to Africa. They roam the land from the Cape to Cairo, so they must be tough survivors. Tradition has it that ostriches will eat almost anything, from natural bush to hay, grain and even old tin cans and bits of discarded cardboard. There should be no problem with feeding the birds.

And, finally, every part of the ostrich is marketable. The leather is in great demand for fashion accessories, the feathers are valued, either as trim for high-fashion garments or as feather dusters, the meat is healthy and cholesterol free, and the bones are used in bone meal. Nothing is wasted.

You just can't lose with ostriches. Or can you?

My grandfather was still farming at Glenelg in the Steynsburg district when he decided to go in for ostriches. In due course six breeding pairs were bought and established in camps near the homestead. Careful study of proper farming methods showed Grandpa that it was best to remove the eggs from the nest and place them in an incubator, so the chicks could be hand-reared.

The advantage of this was that the grown-up birds would regard humans as their parents and tend to be less vicious. Well, that was the theory.

Ostriches are very protective of their eggs, however, and can be very dangerous when aroused. The kick of an ostrich can easily be fatal, as the long, powerful clawed feet are able to rip open a human chest with hardly any effort. Ostriches have a built-in shield of thick bone in their breasts, which protects them in fights. Humans don't.

So the gathering of the eggs had to be planned with military precision.

One of the children would be issued with a bucket of maize and told to walk slowly along the outside of the paddock fence rattling it to attract the adult ostriches.

Once they were following and had moved a safe distance from the nest, Grandpa would pop up from his hiding place, dash into the paddock and grab a couple of eggs from the nest and race for the gate as fast as he could. The ostriches would realise they had been tricked, turn round and gallop back in hot pursuit.

My father, who was usually the bucket-rattler, said it was nail-biting stuff and Grandpa often slammed the gate behind him just in time, and the angry ostriches bounced off it, hissing furiously.

Once the eggs were safely stored in the incubator, they had to be turned each day until the great moment arrived when the first crack appeared in the thick shells and the chicks began to emerge – coffee-coloured, prettily striped with chocolate markings, and covered with short, prickly hair, more like a hedgehog's spikes than feathers.

At first they were kept in a small enclosure and fed regularly with special growing food. Naturally they came to regard people as their source of food and would follow a human whenever one appeared.

As they grew older they would be taken each day to a paddock of lucerne to feed, and returned to their secure sleeping quarters at night. Herding ostriches was a simple business at this stage because they would simply follow anybody from the sleeping pen to the paddock and back. This also caused problems.

My father told me of one occasion when he and his sisters were taking the chicks along the road after a day in the paddock and a horse-drawn cart came rattling by. The chicks saw the people on the cart and decided they should be followed. The cart trundled along happily at trotting pace, with the occupants completely unaware they were being followed by fifty devoted ostrich chicks.

The two young children raced after them all, falling further and further behind and yelling for them to stop, but to no avail.

A horse cart can be a noisy affair.

The whole cavalcade travelled along until they came to a gate across the road, when everything was finally sorted out.

Dad says it took hours to get the chicks home as the sun was setting by that time, and their natural reaction was to settle down to sleep at dusk. The reluctant chicks had to be woken up repeatedly when they settled down in the middle of the road, and chivvied along.

They arrived home long after dark, everybody in a bad mood.

When it was time to pluck the feathers the birds were herded into a small space and a long cloth bag was slipped over their heads to subdue them.

On one occasion the male ostrich, Dirk, managed to peep out of a small hole in the bag. All he could see was Grandpa's pipe, which was in his mouth as he plucked the valuable wing feathers.

Dirk made a sudden lunge, grabbed the pipe in his beak and was about to swallow it when the hot tobacco coals burned his tongue. With a quick shake of the head Dirk sent the pipe spinning through the air, much to the amusement of everybody except Grandpa.

As almost any farmer who has tried ostrich farming will tell you, there's far more to it than meets the eye. My father once said to me, "An ostrich can think up more interesting ways of dying than any other animal I know."

Grandpa's ostrich venture was eventually abandoned and the surviving chicks sold. Only Dirk stayed behind, terrorising anybody who dared stray too close to his paddock. Eventually one fateful day Grandpa was standing near the fence when Dirk sneaked up behind him and gave him a hard peck on the back of his neck. More in surprise than anger, Grandpa swung round and took a swipe at Dirk with his walking stick, hitting him on his long neck.

Dirk promptly collapsed and died, ending an unsuccessful chapter in our family's farming history.

OF DEBTS AND DASSIES

Down at the co-op you'll always hear the latest complaints, as farmers wait to
have their pig meal and laying mash loaded onto their four-by-fours. They'll be
sure to tell you how hard life is these days, and how much unemployment there
is in the country today.

"And inflation! Man, money's worth hardly anything today. I remember
when petrol cost three shillings a gallon. Would you believe that? Thirty
cents for four and a half litres!"

"It's true. You could drive from here to Port Elizabeth for under a pound."

"Ja," they say, shaking their heads mournfully, "things are not what they
used to be."

And of course they're not. They can never be.

But let's not forget that there were far harder times too.

In 1933, during the Great Depression, the world's monetary systems had
collapsed. In Europe desperate people wheeled barrow-loads of worthless
paper money from shop to shop, trying to buy a loaf of bread or a sausage for the
family. In New York stockbrokers hurled themselves from high buildings after
discovering their stocks and bonds were worthless. In South Africa thousands of
unemployed people milled hopelessly in the streets of Johannesburg, looking for
work – anything that would earn them a few shillings.

On Karoo farms the position was just as desperate. In addition to the
Depression, they were enduring the worst drought for many years. Farmers
could no longer pay their workers, but agreed to let them stay on and work in
exchange for their shelter and a little food.

The price of wool dropped so low that it cost more to rail the bales of wool to the market than the price it eventually fetched. Wool farmers simply dumped their lower grade wool in the river in the hope that it would wash away one day when the rains came.

At the height of this misery a gaunt Xhosa figure appeared at my grandfather's door one day, begging for work. All he had was the threadbare blanket on his back. He had walked hundreds of miles from his village in the Transkei looking for work. Grandpa explained that there was not even money to pay his own people, much less to take on an extra hand. The poor man, who was exhausted from his ordeal, said he did not want to be paid. Indeed, he would work on the farm just for the privilege of being allowed to hunt dassies for food in the koppie behind the house.

And so he settled in and helped on the farm part of the time and hunted for his food the rest of the time.

After some months of this subsistence life things began to improve slightly. The rain came and the dassie hunter decided it was time to wend his way home to his family. Grandpa rewarded him for his work by presenting him with a heifer calf, and the man went off leading the young animal, happy and probably feeling richer than he had for many a long month.

And today we complain when there isn't enough money to take the kids to the movies and a steak house! Times – and values – certainly have changed since those hard Depression days. Today most farm labourers live in comfortable homes surrounded by the trappings of modern civilisation.

Not many people would be prepared to eat a dassie these days, let alone agree to accept dassies in lieu of wages.

MATERIAL STUFF

Banzi Ntame's house had burned down. He had been away at a church service on a neighbouring farm when the fire started, probably caused by an electrical fault. Banzi, a long-standing member of the farm staff, who was the choir leader and an enthusiastic church-goer, but not overly endowed with common sense, had more than likely left a kettle or iron switched on.

Whatever the cause, he was now without furniture and we heard there was an auction sale of household goods in the main parking area in Middelburg the following Tuesday. My father allocated a suitable sum of money and we duly set off with Banzi in the farm bakkie, so he could re-furnish his home. All of Middelburg, it seemed, had turned out to watch the sale. A profusion of beds, tables, chairs, boxes of cutlery and crockery, ornaments, kitchen dressers, stoves and fridges were stacked up around the area. Crowds of would-be buyers wandered among the treasure, opening drawers, stroking tabletops, discussing chairs.

"What do you think you need most?" I asked Banzi, shouting above the hubbub.

But his eyes had glazed over and his mind was obviously elsewhere.

"Shall we try bidding for this dining room suite?" I asked.

He looked blank.

"And I guess we'll have to get you a new bed too."

No response.

"Hey," I said, "are you listening to me?"

"How much do you think they'll want for that bird?" he asked, almost in a trance.

"That bird" was a life-size ceramic cockatoo, glazed in lurid shiny pinks, purples and shimmering silver. A truly hideous object, but Banzi was obviously deeply in love with it.

"Bed? Oh yes, I guess I'll need a bed. Any one will do. Yes, those chairs are just fine, just fine. Whatever."

I bid successfully for the furniture I thought he needed, and he accepted that absently, eyeing "that bird" all the time.

Eventually the cockatoo came up for sale and Banzi took over the bidding, waving enthusiastically, hopping from foot to foot. It was knocked down to him for an extortionate price. I'm sure we could have bought half a dozen ceramic cockatoos for the same sum in a shop. But Banzi was a happy man and stood beside it protectively for the rest of the auction sale.

My job done, I found myself sitting on the low wall surrounding the parking area and chatting to the town engineer, Mr Ron Noble.

"I suppose there are quite a number of empty houses in the town now," I ventured. "With the decline in population there must be plenty of houses going for bargain prices." To my surprise he assured me there were no empty houses in the town at all. In fact, prices were rising steadily and anything that came on the market was snapped up fast.

"But surely there are far fewer people in the town now than there were in the 1940s and 1950s? Middelburg used to be absolutely crowded in those days."

"Ah yes," he agreed. "Fewer people, but still as many households as ever."

Not only has the country population dwindled, but it has changed in structure over the years.

"You see," said Mr Noble, "in the old days couples had six or seven children and they all lived together and went to school locally. Then there was usually a grandparent staying with them, or an aged uncle or aunt.

"Quite often, when sons or daughters grew up and married, they lived in the same houses as their parents until they could afford to buy a home of their own.

"It was not unusual for a house to be home to twelve or more people.

"Now families are smaller – one or two kids. Three at most. Granny has moved away to live in a retirement village in the city, so she can play bridge regularly with her old friends.

"People are no longer willing to share their living space with odd relatives. Each family member expects his or her own room. Nobody wants to share any more. So all the houses are occupied, but no longer filled with noisy, interacting relatives."

I suppose it's much the same in the city: smaller families, no hangers-on. More pleasant in one way, I suppose. It's good to have privacy and your own living space. On the other hand, we have lost what was once a vital part of family life – the occupied house.

When Junior comes home from school today both parents are still at work. There always used to be Granny at home to ask about the day's lessons, sit him down to a proper lunch and make sure the homework was done. Now the house is quiet and lonely. Not an inviting place at mid-afternoon. Junior tosses his schoolbooks onto his bed, scratches out a snack of leftovers from the fridge and goes out to look for his friends.

The centre of his social life is now the shopping mall, or the street corner. His manners and standards are those picked up from his peers, not his elders.

It happens throughout the world. We're wealthy, we're living on two incomes, and we have two computers, two cars and the latest electronic games.

Wealthier? Maybe not. We may have more money and more "stuff", but I think we're the poorer for it.

MONEY MAKES THE WORLD GO FLAT

Something sad has happened to our society. We have lost our "respected people".

There was a time not so long ago when every town had its respected people. Among their number you could usually count the dominee, the magistrate, the mayor, the doctor, the school principal, the local attorney and, of course, the bank manager.

Ordinary mortals looked up to these respected people with something approaching reverence.

I remember my father preparing for his annual official visit to the bank manager. It was always a tense time. The bank manager knew all the financial details of every farmer in the district. He alone had the power to grant, or deny, an overdraft, or to foreclose on a farmer who was too deeply in debt.

A powerful man indeed.

No wonder Dad would put on his best suit and his old Grey tie for the visit. Before he set off Mother would make sure the tie was straight and the suit well brushed. This was a serious occasion.

From the bank manager's side, I suppose the annual visit of Norman Biggs was a mere formality. The farm was in sound hands and any financial difficulties were soon cleared up by hard work and careful spending.

But, still, the visit to the bank manager was filled with anxiety and it was always with a relieved sigh that Dad would return home with the pleasing news: "He says the farm's doing well."

Today there are very few bank managers left in small country towns. The branches have been downgraded and are staffed by clerks, possibly under the leadership of an accountant. Even in suburban branches of city banks many managers have only nominal authority. Any real decisions are referred to "head office", which might be in far away Pretoria or Johannesburg.

Besides, most bank transactions are made electronically today. As far as the machine is concerned each customer is just a number and a total. It doesn't make any difference whether you've been a client of the bank for a month or fifty years.

Our bank manager in Noupoort held a special cocktail party when my father had completed fifty years as a client. Speeches were made thanking him for his loyalty and he was presented with a pair of gold cuff links bearing the bank's coat of arms. I can't help wondering how many of today's banks have the slightest idea how long their clients have been with them.

It's probably not considered an important factor.

LET THERE BE LIGHT
(NOISE TOO)

We sit on the terrace in front of my Fish Hoek home and enjoy the stunning view over False Bay, some friends and I, clutching glasses of good Cape wine and chatting quietly about the state of the world.

It's a tranquil enough scene, although the peace is disturbed from time to time by the rumble and roar of a passing lorry or motorbike on the road below.

"You are so lucky to be able to get away from all this city noise," says Carol. "It must be wonderful to be surrounded by all that space and silence in the Karoo."

I wonder to myself whether she really would find the "space and silence" of the Karoo as wonderful as she imagines.

City people are not accustomed to silence – or to darkness.

Even on the quietest suburban night you can hear the muffled hum of traffic a block or two away and see the glow of a street light through the bedroom window. The city is never completely silent, or completely dark.

I was reminded of this not long ago when my son and his children from England were visiting our family farm, Grapevale, on holiday. The sun had set and a light cloud covered the moonless sky. The small boys were having their bedtime bath when the Eskom power failed. This is not an unusual occurrence in the Karoo, where power lines snake their way across many kilometres of bare veld, subject to the wiles of wind and lightning.

The two little boys immediately broke into hysterical shrieks of total panic. Adults groped about for candles and matches, trying all the while to calm the children, but the howls and screams continued at full volume.

It was only when some light was restored that they calmed down again.

It occurred to me that they had just experienced complete darkness for the first time of their lives – a completely alien experience for a city child.

Johannes du Plessis, who farms about ten kilometres away on Macasserfontein, bought the small farm Potfontein next door to him when the owner retired. The farm was purchased simply to add a bit more grazing land to Macasserfontein, but there was a fine farmstead included in the deal, complete with duck pond, sheds and a comfortable small house.

It seemed a pity simply to allow it all to fall into ruin. Johannes decided to rent it as a peaceful little holiday cottage where city people could get away from the bustle and racket for a while and recharge their spiritual batteries.

Advertisements appeared in the city newspapers and it was not long before the first city folk arrived in their smart car, eager to escape civilisation for a while. They were shown around the house and told how to operate the electric generator, gas fridge and water heater. The fridge was packed with wholesome fresh farm fare, crisply ironed sheets covered the beds and firewood was stacked in the grate in case of chilly night weather.

They were left to their peace and tranquillity.

Early the next morning Johannes arrived to ensure that his guests were comfortable, only to find the screen door firmly shut and an envelope pinned to it.

Inside was payment for a night's accommodation and a terse little note that said: "Sorry. We could not stand the silence, so we have gone back to Johannesburg."

Apparently they'd packed the car and left shortly after midnight.

When last did you experience complete silence?

In modern cities every silence is deliberately smothered with noise. In restaurants and shops, from passing cars and in shopping malls, electronic muzak is squirted into our ears twenty-four hours a day.

There's a medical condition known as "Boilermaker's Deafness", where the sufferer cannot hear anything unless it is accompanied by a background clatter of noise. Could it be that the modern world is suffering from an acute case of collective boilermaker's deafness?

RAINBIRDS

The early 1930s were harsh years throughout the world, as the Great Depression gripped country after country. Fortunes were lost, and millionaires in London and Paris found themselves paupers overnight. In the arid Karoo the farmers looked in vain at the steel-silver sky day after day, willing the rain to come.

On our farm there was a lonely outpost far from the farmhouse, where Tobias, the shepherd, spent his solitary days watching the flocks and gathering them into a stone kraal at night as protection against marauding jackals and lynxes.

One burning day Tobias arrived unexpectedly at the farmhouse and stood outside, respectfully clutching his battered hat in his hands.

My grandfather wondered what had occasioned this rare visit.

"Oubaas," said Tobias, after the usual polite preliminaries, "I think it is time we brought the rain. The sheep cannot live much longer without water."

Well, that seemed a reasonable idea. All that was needed was the way to make it rain. Did Tobias have any suggestions?

"Yes, Oubaas," he said. "We will need a hamerkop."

The hamerkop (*Scopus umbretta*) is a strange, large-headed bird that builds a vast, untidy nest at the top of a cliff, or krans, adding to it annually. All sorts of scraps and rubbish can be found within the tangled mess of a hamerkop's nest – old pieces of clothing, tin cans, wire, even a perished bicycle tyre – all lovingly transported to the cliff-top and tucked among the twigs and leaves.

The hamerkop is always found near water, as it feeds mainly on frogs and other aquatic creatures. Hamerkops are regarded as interesting but harmless. Nobody would shoot one in the normal course of events.

But here was Tobias, suggesting that a dead hamerkop could be used to bring the rain. My father, Norman, was a young man then, just out of school and starting to learn the complexities of being a farmer under the guidance of my grandfather, oubaas Clem Biggs.

More to humour old Tobias than in any hope of bringing rain, he was sent off with his rifle and in due course returned, feeling rather guilty, but bringing a dead hamerkop.

"Now we must make haste," said Tobias, "because there is not much water left in the spruit."

Indeed, the spring that fed a trickle of water into the riverbed had almost dried up, something that had not happened in living memory.

Over the last small muddy puddle Tobias suspended the dead bird from the branch of a willow tree, using a length of leather thong. Its head lay forlornly in the mud. Under the scorching sky Tobias set off back to his flock, followed, as always, by his faithful dog, panting in the heat.

The next day a few small clouds appeared on the horizon. Slowly they spread and turned from white to grey and from grey to deep purplish black. Thunder rolled across the sky and the first great drops of water raised puffs of dust from the parched earth.

The rains had come at last.

Trickles turned to streams and streams joined hands to become rivers.

Frogs clicked and chuckled in the mud, sheep huddled for shelter under the last few bushes left by the drought. Great muddy torrents swirled along the riverbeds, washing away topsoil. The family watched in appreciation from the shelter of the farmhouse stoep.

For four days it rained continuously and hard.

Then, from out of the sheets of water appeared the bedraggled form of Tobias, his threadbare blanket drawn over his old shoulders.

When he had reached the shelter of the stoep he removed his sodden hat and said, "Oubaas, I think we must stop it raining now or the veld will wash away."

Grandpa agreed, but asked ruefully how the rain could be stopped.

Tobias splashed away in the direction of the river. Some time later he returned, clutching what remained of the hamerkop.

"The crabs have eaten its head," he announced solemnly. "It will still rain for two more days."

And of course, as happens in all good stories, his prophecy came true. Two days later the rain abated. The puddles dried up, the rivers became streams again and the streams became sandy watercourses once more.

In later years, whenever a drought became too hard to bear, family members would say (only half in jest), "Maybe we should go out and shoot a hamerkop."

They never did. Hamerkops are harmless old birds.

Some might say that a man like Tobias – who spent his days under the sparse shade of a *besembos* watching the sheep graze, and his nights under the open canopy of stars – would know about the weather and be able to feel in his bones what was about to happen.

Others might know that the sacrifice of a hamerkop could bring rain.

There are, after all, many things that even modern science cannot explain.

THERE IS SOME CORNER OF A FOREIGN FIELD THAT IS FOREVER ENGLAND

There's hardly any part of the Great Karoo that was not a battlefield at some time or another during the long and senseless South African War.

Sturdy concrete block-houses built by British Army engineers dot the landscape still, where vital railway lines needed to be protected from swift Boer commandos who could strike fast and vanish like ghosts into the familiar veld while the British troops struggled with unfamiliar heat, disease and homesickness.

In my home village of Noupoort the British troops stationed there built an attractive stone Anglican church that is now a national monument, but untended and in a state of sad neglect.

There are not many Anglicans in Noupoort.

Nearby Middelburg was the site of a huge British military camp, mostly used as a remount station where tired horses and mules could be rested and exchanged for fresh mounts. Most of the barrack buildings were later incorporated in the well-known Grootfontein Agricultural College, where many of the most successful sheep farmers in the region were trained.

The little hamlet of Matjiesfontein near Laingsburg was also a British remount station where more than ten thousand British troops were stationed, living in precise rows of white army tents and looking after up to twelve thousand horses.

Take time to stop and look at the grey stretches of bare veld and the harsh dolerite koppies and imagine what it must have looked like to the nineteen-year-old British soldiers used to the lush green rolling hills of Sussex, dotted with friendly little villages every few miles.

They must have thought they'd landed in Hell.

Near almost every little Karoo town British forces set up their neat and ordered military camps, with row upon straight row of snow-white tents. The railways were vital for the transport of men and equipment across the barren plains.

British Officers dressed formally for dinner even in the heat of summer and the formality of Victorian England was maintained at all costs, no matter how far from dear old Blighty they happened to be.

I am told that General Redvers Buller never travelled anywhere during the war without his piano. One has to retain the finer things of life, even in battle. I marvel at the thought of the effort and manpower that piano must have cost the British Army.

"The definition of a gentleman," my maternal grandmother from Nottinghamshire used to tell me, "is someone who uses a butter knife even when he dines alone."

The British officers may have been pompous fools and idiots, but they certainly were gentlemen.

The Boer forces, in complete contrast, were rough, tough men of the veld. They knew the rocky koppies and ravines well, rode hard and struck unexpectedly, only to vanish swiftly into the grey countryside, leaving the frustrated Brits angry and confused.

Driving through the Karoo one can easily imagine the feelings of confusion and hopelessness that must have overcome the young British soldiers from Suffolk and Gloucestershire.

Colesberg, one of the closest towns to our family farm, has an interesting museum in which the South African War features prominently. Its curator Belinda Gordon has studied the battles that rolled around the town and recounts some heart-rending personal stories gleaned from letters of young soldiers during that war.

In 1899 Private H Potter (could this be the original Harry Potter?) of the 1st Suffolk's wrote to his previous employer Mr Petit, coach builder in Bury St Edmonds, about his first impressions on arrival in South Africa:

"I was not much struck by Cape Town, what little I did see of it from our ship whilst in harbour, as it was our only chance, for as soon as we landed we were served with 1 000 rounds of ammunition, packed into a train that was standing quite close to the quay, and away to the front, it seemed so sudden we could hardly believe it.

"We soon lost sight of Cape Town, and we were all wondering where we were going to, but still we kept passing station after station till night came on, but still we kept running on. We all fell asleep at last and the next morning when we awoke we were still going. We found out where we were going when we reached De Aar station (about 700 miles from Cape Town.) We were heading for Naauwport and we reached it early next morning after being nearly 50 hours on the train."

Private Potter did not   k much of the Cape, and who could blame him?

"I could not help noticing the Cape Colony was a desolate place," he wrote. "There being scarcely any inhabitants whatsoever."

(Maybe it's rather unfair to judge the whole Cape Colony from the point of view of Noupoort, but that was his impression, understandably.)

Around the same time a Private Bridges wrote to his wife in Bury St Edmonds: "You would look if you could see me. I have not had a chance to wash for three days and we have not had our boots off for a week, so we are getting some of the hard times. I think we shall be glad when it is all over."

One of the most disastrous battles of the war, for the British Army, was fought near Colesberg on a hill that is still known as Suffolk Hill. It took place in the very early hours of January the 6th, 1900.

The British decided it was necessary to capture the grassy koppie near the town. The 1st Suffolk Regiment were detailed to storm the hill before dawn. Independently another regiment, made up of South African troops, had also decided the hill should be taken. The two parties met and clashed with horrible slaughter, but only after Boer commandos had wrought terrible havoc with their Mauser fire from the shelter of the rocky koppie.

Belinda kindly sent me copies of the letters written afterwards by British survivors. They tell the story better than dry history books could do.

Private J Ruffles wrote home: "I was one of the lucky ones on 6th January, which I dare say you know about. There were about 330 of our regiment went to take a hill with 3 or 4 thousand Boers on it. I with my Company had been laying on the hills for four days opposite the Boers, firing at each other. We got relieved at 6 in the morning for a day's rest. At bedtime that night orders came that we were to parade at 4.00 am in the morning to attack the hill. We were to march up, wait a short distance from it and fix bayonets at daybreak. The artillery would shell the enemy position for one hour, then we were to charge the hill and fire as much as we like, so as to take them by surprise and drive them out. The cavalry were there to cut them off at the right flank and the mounted infantry at the left. These were our orders and no doubt it would have proved a great success. Instead we were called at midnight and paraded in our slippers."

In their soft footwear the poor exhausted troops started to climb the rocky koppie. Another soldier takes up the story:

"The hill was covered with huge boulders and the men had to assist one another to climb up which proved very fatiguing.

"Every now and then the troops halted to listen. They were nearly at the top of the hill when the invisible 'night bird' again gushed forth its dulcet tones, to be followed almost immediately by a rifle shot fired by a Boer sentry, who was discovered

standing by himself just in front of the leading company and just in front of the centre of the hill. He was immediately bayoneted by one of our men and the column lay down among the rocks waiting a few seconds.

"Then the hill was ablaze with rifle fire. Mauser and explosive bullets dropping among our men in showers. Nearly all the poor chaps and officers who were at the front got knocked down and the Colonel was wounded. He came back a little way and said, 'Retire my men,' and those in the front companies kept knocking us down in the rear. Our chaps got stabbed with our own bayonets as we could hardly see one another. When we got back to camp only one officer, Major Graham, got back; he was wounded in two places. A little later a fellow came in and said our artillery was firing into our own men and did not know it.

"We were relieved by the 'Essex' and sent back to Naaupoort."

(Major Graham was shot through his right arm and lung. He somehow escaped capture and crawled almost two miles back to camp.)

The tattered remnant of the regiment was withdrawn to Port Elizabeth to recover and await a fresh intake of officers.

A Mr Forbes Grant's letter ends by giving his reasons for the Suffolk's defeat. He probably hits the nail firmly on the head.

"Each Boer is a fighting unit; now each Tommy is not. Each Boer is left to his own resources; he takes his own position; he retreats when he thinks fit and chooses his own line of flight. Tommy can't do that. He is part of his section or his company: he must do as he is told, and if there is no one to tell him what to do he is in a bad way."

Anybody contemplating starting a war should be required to visit the museums of the Karoo. There they would learn, sooner than elsewhere, of the total stupidity and wastefulness of any war.

There are no winners. Only losers and survivors.

WAR ON THE PLAINS

The declaration of war in 1939 found the Karoo deeply divided. Old wounds heal slowly in rural communities, and the bitter divide between Boer and Brit still rankled thirty years after the South African War had officially ended.

At the start of the war a recruitment office was established in Colesberg and many of the English-speaking farmers answered the call to war. A substantial number of Afrikaners felt more sympathy with Germany and joined clandestine organisations like the Ossewa Brandwag. Years after World War II, I remember discussions in which the family described neighbours as "loyal" or otherwise, "loyal" meaning they'd sided with General Smuts in support of the Allied side.

In our district the young pro-British farmers got together soon after General Jannie Smuts had officially committed South Africa to fighting for the Allies. Most of the unmarried men – or those without children – chose to volunteer for active service. My grandfather, Clement Biggs, decreed that my father should stay behind to look after the farm, as well as those of some others who had volunteered. My father, Norman, joined the newly-established Home Guard regiment and was assigned five farms to manage for the duration of the war.

Three of my aunts – Elma, Rhona and May – joined up as nurses and were sent, after training, to serve with the Allied forces in Egypt. Uncle Llewellyn from Graaff-Reinet joined Die Middellandse Regiment.

Uncle Douglas Rogers (my mother's brother) joined the Police Brigade and later became a despatch rider and was seriously wounded. His wounds never healed completely and he suffered from their effects right up to his death, more than fifty years later.

Uncle Neville Howes, who was married to Aunt Elma and lived on the farm Kenilworth, next to ours, joined the air force and served as a rear gunner in a bomber squadron. He was killed tragically right at the end of the war.

Obviously, as a three- and four-year-old, I had no idea what all this talk of war was about. My earliest memories are of the family huddled round the elegant wooden cabinet of the Pye radio ("the wireless" to us) every lunchtime, listening to the world news broadcast. Each advance or retreat was discussed at great length. From my vantage point at adult knee height I could sense that these were solemn times.

One of the daily tasks was to ensure that the car battery that powered the radio was checked and swopped with the tractor battery when the charge was low.

Home Guard parades were held at the show grounds in Colesberg every second Friday and seemed to entail a great deal of polishing of buttons and buckles. Dad was a sergeant and the regiment was under the command of Major Jack Garlake, the local attorney.

At first there were no rifles available for members of the HG, and they learned rifle drill using crude wooden cutouts or even walking sticks and broom handles. Later they were issued with real rifles – long-service Lee Enfields – and held regular target practice at the rifle range, which was situated a few miles from the town. My father often told the story of his acute embarrassment when, during a target practice, his five-year-old son (me) asked what made the targets go up and down after each shot was fired. Overhearing my question, the commanding officer issued an unusual order.

"Sergeant Biggs," he barked, "take your son and explain to him how the targets work."

In front of the whole regiment, a red-faced Sergeant Biggs shouldered his five-year-old son and marched the five hundred metres to the targets.

I can remember being taken down some steps into a pit area below the targets and shown how the position of each shot was signalled to the shooter by means of a black disc on a long pole that was held in front of the bullet hole. The targets could be rolled up into the firing position, or down into the pit for repairs. Patches of the appropriate colour were applied to the targets as they became too heavily perforated.

The .303 ammunition was in great demand and one officer was always designated to sit firmly on the ammunition box to prevent pilfering.

I later heard of some of the outrageous tricks the men employed to remove that officer from his box for the few seconds needed to grab a handful of bullets.

On one occasion the guard corporal suddenly found himself being attacked by a swarm of those fierce little black army ants that can bite like the very devil. The South African Army uniform at the time included short pants, and the insects soon found tender spots to attack. The corporal leapt from his box, slapping madly at his thighs. Several helpful soldiers joined in, swatting enthusiastically.

Others moved the ammunition box away from the ants' nest and set it down in a safer place (slightly lighter than before). Somebody remarked it was odd that they had never seen army ants round the shooting range before.

Afterwards in the pub an officer asked, "Hey, Charley, how did you arrange those ants, man?"

"Me?" said the indignant Charley, taking his battered cigarette tin from his battledress pocket. "I know nothing about ants." And he looked into the tin and sighed, "Oh, damn, I seem to have run out of fags. Anybody got one for me?" As he lit the proffered cigarette, he emptied the remaining grains of sugar from the tin into the ashtray on the bar counter.

During the war years, when arms and ammunition were obviously strictly controlled, the springbok herds on all the farms multiplied and increased until they became a real problem, competing for the available grazing with the farm stock.

With five farms to look after, my parents were kept very busy.

My mother qualified as a wool classer and I remember her pride when she was awarded her official "Springbok Head" stencil. When this was applied to a bale of wool it indicated that the contents had been sorted and graded by a qualified wool classer and the buyer could be assured of the consistency of the wool inside. Not many women achieved this distinction.

My father fitted a metal seat to the back of our big green Massey-Harris tractor, and I was toted along from farm to farm when there was ploughing or harvesting to be done. My mother, who came from a horse-breeding background, was delighted to have the use of a particularly good horse on the farm Fonteintjie, belonging to Meiring van Niekerk. She delighted in riding from place to place, checking the water supplies for the stock and seeing that fences were in order.

Granny Biggs was an enthusiastic knitter and many South African lads must have been pleased to receive some of her vast output of knitted jerseys and socks that went off in Red Cross parcels for "our boys up north".

My next clear wartime memory was when it all ended and news was received that the district's men were coming home.

Excited wives and relatives gathered at our farm and rolled out a long banner of red crepe paper. On it, in letters made of white glued-on cotton wool, they wrote: "Welcome Home". It was strung up along the Noupoort station platform shortly before the troop train was due to arrive. I remember tears and laughter and hugs, as the aunties I knew so well embraced these strange men in uniform. One of them didn't seem to have an aunty to hug, so I went up and gave him a big welcome hug. I was five years old. Obviously this must have left a lasting impression, as Meiring van Niekerk always treated me with special kindness afterwards.

One of the first tasks that faced the returning soldiers was to reduce the numbers of springbok on their farms. Ammunition was again available and large hunts were organised.

It was a massacre. In a family photograph album there's a faded picture of more than one hundred dead springbok lined up neatly in the farmyard.

The buck were put to good use, though – taken to Noupoort station with tickets tied to their horns, and railed to Port Elizabeth, Durban and Cape Town, where they were sold to raise money for the Red Cross.

The organisation was fully employed dealing with the aftermath of the war and needed all the financial help it could get. Hundreds of men returned from active service or POW camps physically or mentally damaged. In the icy Karoo winter there was no need for cold storage for the springbok carcasses during the journey.

It was fifty years later, at my father's funeral in Middelburg, that I learned one more fact about those wartime years.

As the mourners stood forlornly outside the church, a farmer, whom I knew only vaguely, came up and said to me: "I don't know whether you ever knew this but, when those men returned from the war, every one of the farms your father looked after had had all its debts wiped out. Their bonds were paid and there wasn't a single pound owing on any of them."

There are more ways of serving than shouldering arms.

Going Walkabout
and the Philosophy of Lucerne

Whenever the pressures and routines of city life crowd in too oppressively, I load a small pack on my old motorcycle and head away into the saner reaches of the countryside to be alone for a few days of freedom and mental recharging.

The Australian aboriginals call this "going walkabout" and consider it an essential part of life.

The first thing I leave behind is an itinerary. As the days pass I settle down to a more leisurely routine, waking at dawn, loading the bike and cruising quietly along empty gravel roads lined with dew-heavy grass until a suitable breakfast venue rolls into view. Long dreamy pauses under a handy peppercorn tree, watching springbok graze, quiet conversations with farmers under the pretext of asking the way (as if it matters when there's no fixed destination).

One day in the 1970s I pointed my 500cc Yamaha thumper northwards and rode through Malmesbury and Riebeek Kasteel, going faster and faster, as always happens on the first day of a walkabout – it's almost as though I am fleeing the snapping jaws of the noisome city.

It must have been somewhere near Prince Alfred Hamlet that I rode into a vast swarm of locusts on that first day. Anybody who has driven through a locust swarm in a car will know what a frightening experience it can be.

On a motorcycle it's even more interesting.

Suddenly the sky was dark with the whirring, clicking insects and they clattered against the visor of my helmet, exploding into a horrible yellow mess. My scruffy leather jacket was coated with the goo and pieces of leg and wing adhered to the sticky juices.

To escape this nightmare I took the first turn-off and headed eastward, aiming for... well, anywhere, as long as it was far from those locusts.

Once clear of them, I stopped at the roadside and scraped off the worst of the mess, and again at a farm dam to wash some more off the visor.

After some hours of fast riding I arrived in the village of Jansenville.

Now Jansenville was home to one of the most interesting characters of the Karoo, an attorney called Sid Fourie. Sid was an old bachelor who had done great deeds of generosity to the people of the town. He had anonymously paid for several deserving young children to go on overseas school tours they could never have afforded, and he was one of the founders of the local hospital and a regular contributor to its coffers. Highly respected by all, he wrote several books of short pieces about the people of the town, published them privately and gave copies to the people he had mentioned.

This slightly-built, wrinkled man had handled some of the family's legal matters and, although I had never met him, I'd heard a great deal about him and decided to look him up. Everybody in the dorp knew where Oom Sid Fourie lived and I soon found myself on his doorstep, knocking politely.

When he opened the door his eyes widened and he greeted me with the less than welcoming: *"Wie die hel is jy?"* (Who the hell are you?)

Not that I could blame him, as I was still rather locust infested and coated with dust.

I explained that I was Oom Norman Biggs's son and he looked me up and down critically as I picked a locust leg from my beard.

"When I was young," he said, "I used to go to Sunday school where they taught me about John the Baptist who lived in the desert and ate locusts. And I formed a picture in my mind of exactly what John the Baptist looked like. *Net soos jy, jou bogger!"* (Just like you, you bugger!)

But he invited me in and offered me a drink and we were soon chatting amiably. One of his favourite subjects was the way the Karoo was being ruined by farmers who insisted on planting crops and pumping out the precious underground water to irrigate them.

"Lucerne," he snorted. "It's the worst weed in the Karoo. The farmers plough up valuable, hardy Karoo veld to plant bleddy lucerne. They set up big pumps to suck the earth dry. What a tragedy! The springs are drying up and the windmills will soon run dry too."

I felt rather guilty because we had once had many hectares of land planted to lucerne on Grapevale. What a business that was!

First there was the expensive machinery needed to grow and harvest the lucerne. A tractor fitted with a mower, a wide side-delivery rake to gather the cut lucerne into windrows, and a baling machine to press it into tight bales. Then there was the trailer to carry it safely into the shed for storage. All this needed a great deal of heavy manual labour in the hot sun.

There was also the problem of bloat.

Lucerne is dried before being used as highly nutritious stock feed. While it is growing in the field it can be quite toxic and cause bloat if animals eat it green.

Sometimes a gate would be left open and a herd of cows would wander in to eat the tempting green leaves and find themselves in great pain.

It is not a pretty sight.

The juices of the green lucerne react with the stomach juices of the cows to produce a huge volume of gas. Before long there's a whole herd of cows standing about looking like balloons and burping. In extreme cases they fall down and some of them die.

The cure that was used was rather a violent one. A short dagger-like instrument called a trocar would be plunged into the bloated animal's tummy to leave a vent hole through which the smelly gas could escape, together with noxious green bubbles. Obviously the animal felt pretty rotten for some days afterwards as the puncture healed.

Later somebody discovered that a wine bottle of old motor oil forced down the bloated cow's throat did the trick, causing it to belch and fart alarmingly, releasing the gas without requiring a punctured gut.

Either way, it was all rather a lot of bother.

One year we had a particularly good crop of lucerne and at the end of summer it was all stacked away safely in a huge shed at the far end of the farm, ready for the next drought.

Every time we looked at that shed we had a smug feeling of superiority. You could feed all the stock on the farm for a whole winter on that lot.

Then one quiet Sunday afternoon somebody spotted a column of smoke rising from the lucerne shed, and everybody boarded the truck and raced up to see what was happening. We arrived just in time to watch the last of the rafters collapse into the ashes.

A family of vagrants, who were now disappearing hastily over the horizon, had apparently moved into the shed and settled down on the soft hay, not thinking that their cooking fire might set the whole lot alight.

Dad's enthusiasm for lucerne waned after that, and the machinery was sold and the lands were allowed to return to tough old Karoo vegetation that needs no irrigation or mowing and attracts no vagrants.

Dad later said he could have bought all the lucerne in the Swartland for the amount of money he spent annually on machinery, fuel and labour to grow enough to make a few pathetic bales of the stuff.

Nature has a way of surviving almost any setbacks, even the stupidity of man. The best thing a farmer can do is ask himself: "How would this work if I were not here to mess it up?" and try to follow that pattern as closely as possible. After all, the Karoo got along perfectly well for millennia without boreholes or lucerne.

THE KAROO -
FOUNTAINS OF WISDOM

Strangers to the Karoo are sometimes puzzled by the number of farms named after fountains.

In our area – around Colesberg and Middelburg – there's Potfontein, Jakkalsfontein, Tweefontein, Fonteintjie, Raasfontein, Blydefontein and a whole host of other "fonteins".

Before you start thinking of the Karoo as a place of spouting, splashing fountains, like the gardens of the Palace of Versailles in France, remember that the English word for this kind of fountain is a spring.

All over the Karoo, tucked away in hidden valleys and the folds of ironstone koppies, you'll find little natural springs, where mineral-rich water comes seeping out of the rocks. Sometimes it trickles for just a few metres before being swallowed up by the warm riverbed sand. Some springs form rock pools, where for centuries dassies and buck have come each evening to drink.

There are some springs that have never dried up in living memory. They support noisy populations of frogs and tiny aquatic insects in ponds surrounded by reeds, and provide drinking water for a wide variety of animals and birds.

Most of the Karoo fauna have adapted to a lifestyle that requires very little water for survival.

The one exception is Modern Man.

Man is a water-hungry animal, whether in the cities or out on the dry plains of the Karoo. Even in today's enlightened age, municipalities find it almost impossible to persuade residents that their water supplies are not unlimited.

We're a wasteful race.

Wherever the early settlers found a source of natural water, they established a farm and named it after their water source. Kuilfontein produced enough water to form little pools, or "kuils". At Brakfontein the water was brackish and at Raasfontein ("noisy spring") the water made a bubbling sound as it oozed from the rocks. But the settler farmers wanted more water than that supplied by their springs. They dug boreholes and discovered what appeared to be limitless sources of underground water not far below the surface.

Many farmers immediately set up mechanical pumping plants and established irrigated fields of wheat and lucerne.

They flourished for a while. Then the underground water supplies started to diminish. Farmers blamed the droughts. The lucerne and wheat withered and the fields turned to dust bowls.

What was worse, the natural springs began to dry up.

Tweefontein no longer had two fountains. Not even one. Raasfontein fell silent. The pump engines were dismantled and sold, or left to rust.

And gradually, one by one, the fountains began to trickle again.

Memories are long in the country and good farmers don't make the same mistake twice. They've learned that the Karoo treats those well who treat the land with respect.

Today every farm camp has its windmill. Windmills should be the emblem of the Karoo. These slow-moving, efficient machines operate only when the wind blows. And then they gently lift a mere cup-full of water with every stroke of the pump. The water troughs fill up and the stock has drinking water.

There's enough for all, but only enough.

Try to plunder that precious underground supply and the Karoo metes out its punishment by closing down her generous fountains.

Good farmers have learned to work with Nature. They live in quiet harmony with their surroundings, taking no more than they need.

Greedy farmers eventually have to move away and can be found in the cities, working as sales people or handymen and wondering why the Karoo treated them so harshly.

THE NOBLE ANIMAL

In the Colesberg district the farming community is divided between the sheep farmers and the horse breeders.

I'm told the mineral-rich underground water in the area promotes healthy bone growth in horses and many of the winners of the Durban July Handicap in KwaZulu-Natal and the Cape's Metropolitan Handicap owe their success to the boreholes of the Karoo.

Our family have always been sheep farmers, and we tended to look with suspicion at the thoroughbred horse people. We've always felt there's something not completely kosher about the racehorse business. Sheep farmers raise sheep for wool and meat, and sell the results of their labour on the open market at prices determined by supply and demand. It's a straightforward operation. All above board. When prices are high the sheep farmers smile. When prices drop you see grim faces on the streets of Colesberg and Middelburg. That's life.

Things are a bit different with the horse breeders. Their lives seemed to us simple sheep folk to be very convoluted. On Saturday afternoons at the tennis club the horsey people behaved rather strangely. They'd suddenly look at their watches in the middle of a game, drop their racquets and make a rush for their parked cars, to turn on the Supersonic radio and hear the results of the latest race at Turffontein in Gauteng or Kenilworth in Cape Town.

Then there would be cheers and backslapping, or mournful commiserations, depending on the outcome.

And to us sheep farmers none of it made much sense. It might be a horse from Hanover or Aberdeen that won the race, but this would apparently mean thousands of rands of profit to Uncle Archy Dell or Uncle Alex Robertson in Colesberg because the winning horse happened to be the second cousin to the sire of one of the Colesberg horses.

How this made the neighbours rich we never could understand.

Then there was the mysterious matter of the "TJ" cars that were always appearing at stud farms (before the invention of GP licence plates all Johannesburg cars bore the TJ registration letters).

If we saw a foreign car parked outside a sheep farmer's house we'd know straight away that it was the rep for Cooper's dip or Valbazine worm remedy, or the agent from the BKB meat co-op.

Straightforward stuff.

But those long flat Jo'burg cars – Cadillacs, Jaguars and Mercedes Benzes and the like – contained very suspicious types who wore ties and smelled strongly of after-shave "poeftesous". Some of them owned half shares in a stallion that was on loan to the local breeder in return for a quarter share in the future winnings of the progeny. Others apparently wanted to check out which horses were worth a few thousand rands in bets.

Very tricky stuff to us simple sheep chaps.

Personally, I never understood the attraction of horses.

We all grew up with farm horses and rode regularly as part of farm life. It always seemed a highly overrated pastime to me.

There was the matter of catching the stupid thing, for a start. I must have wasted thousands of boy-hours trying to sneak up on my horse and slip a bridle over its head. The horse would stand there, all innocent and docile, flicking its ears idly at passing flies, until the bridle was almost over its head, then toss its silly head, neigh derisively and trot off to the furthest corner of the field. After half an hour of this wasteful occupation the horse would eventually be snared and brought back to the stables to have its saddle fitted.

Everybody who has messed about with horses will tell you that a horse's favourite trick is to inflate its tummy when you try to tighten the girth. This means that, as soon as you place a foot in the stirrup, the loose saddle slides round and lands up under the horse's belly.

Horses find this immensely amusing.

But we all know that horses are *noble* animals, so we're not allowed to give them a swift kick in the ribs, which is the normal human reaction.

Eventually the whole assembly would be road-ready, and we'd set off at a reluctant trot down the road for an hour's ride. I don't think our horses ever got into the spirit of the exercise, as they kept looking longingly over their shoulders at the road home, and shying at innocent things like ant-heaps or meerkats in a half-hearted attempt to unseat us.

It took some coaxing to achieve any more than a slow trot. The ride home was always completely different. The horses sensed that freedom was at hand and shot off at break-neck speed on the home stretch. All we could do was hang on tightly. Our regular rides took an hour outward and five minutes to return.

Then there was the matter of "walking your horse cool". Apparently hot horses need to be wound down gently, so we were required to walk them about slowly to cool off after their terrible exertion (hah!).

One horse in particular – my brother's horse, Shadow – had a really nasty habit during this exercise. We'd walk the horses to a small dam near the garden, where they could have a nice drink after the ride. And Shadow would always want to go one more step into the water, and another step and another, while drinking all the while, head down. Then he would quietly lie down and roll in the muddy water, tipping his unfortunate rider into the mud.

But horses are *noble* animals and we're not allowed to kick them in the ribs, as I think I said before.

Riding always seemed to consist of a great deal of sweat and struggle for a very small amount of actual transported progress. I notice that modern sheep farms are all equipped with efficient little off-road motorcycles that require no catching or grooming, and can be put back in the shed without running them slowly around the yard to cool off. And they very seldom lie down in the mud, either.

"If God had meant us to ride horses," my late father used to say, "He wouldn't have created motorbikes." And I agree with all my heart.

The fame of Colesberg's horses goes back a long way.

Even before the town was named, and the area was still known as the "Cis-Gariep" ("this side of the Gariep River", which was later called the Orange River and is now Gariep again), the horses in the district had acquired an almost mystical reputation. In her book, *The Microcosm*, Dr Thelma Gutsche describes one of the horses' feats of stamina.

"The Cape horse was remarkable for its strength and endurance," she writes. "In 1823, Thompson rode 56 miles in one day, 'the last 30 at full gallop on a sturdy African pony saddled for me fresh from the pasturage,' which, he said, would have killed any English horse."

Another interesting attribute of the Cis-Gariep horses was their legendary homing instinct. Apparently they could find their way home over enormous distances. Unscrupulous horse traders used this to good effect. Sometimes they would sell a horse to a buyer from far away, confident that the animal would eventually find its way home, ready to be sold again.

In *Karoo Morning* Guy Butler tells the story of James Collett of the farm Grassridge in the Cradock district.

The Colletts were enthusiastic horse breeders and trainers.

In 1854 James was elected as a member of the first Legislative Assembly, which met in Cape Town, about six hundred and fifty miles away (one thousand and forty kilometres). In those days there were no fat perks for politicians as there are today. Members served out of a sense of duty and honour and were expected to pay their own expenses. After riding all the way to Cape Town, James scouted about for suitable stabling for his horses, but felt that the prices quoted by greedy Cape stable owners were simply outrageous. In fact, he worked out that the price he would have to pay to keep his horses stabled for the duration of the assembly's session was more than the price of two new horses.

The Colletts were all known as thrifty people, loath to part with a penny unless it was absolutely necessary, so James took his horses to the outskirts of the city and simply turned them loose.

When the session ended he bought two new horses to carry him home and, when he arrived, there were his original mounts waiting for him. The story has it that they had taken just fifteen days to travel from the Cape to Cradock.

That's an average of seventy kilometres a day, which isn't bad going.

THE MAGIC OF KAROO MUTTON

This is probably not a good chapter for squeamish readers, or those who believe meat comes ready wrapped from supermarket shelves.

If that's you, maybe you should skip it.

Most city people will agree: there's no meat to compare with Karoo lamb. The sad thing is that hardly anybody in the city has actually experienced the flavour of real Karoo lamb.

Don't be fooled by the neatly packaged stuff you see in the supermarket coolers marked "Karoo Lamb". It may have come from the Karoo, but there's not likely to be much of the proper flavour left by the time it reaches the Styrofoam tray.

There's a simple reason for this – adrenalin. The poor animal has probably spent a whole day being bounced about on the back of a three-decker lorry, then stood for a whole fear-filled day in the crowded stockyards at the city abattoir, surrounded by other frightened animals and the smell of death everywhere.

Its panicked system pumps out so much adrenalin that it's about all you taste when you finally get it onto your dinner table. Back in the country the sheep is grazing peacefully in the veld, and half an hour later it's been slaughtered, skinned and hung up in a cold room. It simply hasn't had time to be scared.

Karoo mutton gets its wonderful herbal flavour from eating the tough little Karoo bushes that smell rather like rosemary. That should be the flavour you get.

I remember one rather unpleasant day when a sheep was brought into the yard for slaughter and escaped from the back of the truck. In panic it ran about being chased by the whole farm staff, all shouting instructions, waving their arms and falling about like idiots.

Round the back of the cowshed they all galloped, then back into the yard and down the front drive, then back into the yard again, all hollering and whooping.

Eventually the sheep was caught and slaughtered.

The meat tasted so dreadful that even the farm dogs rejected it.

None of this will be news to stock farmers. In fact, they did try to improve matters a few years ago, but big money spoiled everything, as it so often does. (Look what it's done to sport.)

As in so many industries, the people who make the big money from meat are not the farmers who produce it, or the butchers who sell it. It's all the clever people in between: the agents, the wholesalers and all the others who grab their slice without ever going near a sheep or leg of lamb.

A number of stock farmers in the Colesberg district decided the present system of meat marketing was all wrong. The main problem lay, they thought, with the long journey the animals had to endure before reaching the market. The solution seemed so obvious it was amazing nobody had suggested it before.

It went like this.

Set up professional, modern abattoirs in the small country towns, slaughter the animals there and transport the carcasses to the city in refrigerated trucks.

Think of the benefits. The meat tastes ten times better for the consumer. You can transport far more carcasses in a cooled lorry than you can live animals. They don't get bruised and bumped once they're loaded as carcasses, so the meat arrives in perfect condition.

And – this is very important – the country abattoirs would provide much needed jobs and relieve some of the overcrowding in the big cities.

You have to admit it's hard to find a flaw in the idea.

After navigating mountains of red tape it was agreed that a trial run would be undertaken. One consignment of meat was to be sent to each of the main centres to see whether the scheme would work as well as the farmers thought it would.

Expensive refrigerated trucks were hired, the animals were slaughtered and the carcasses loaded. One truck was destined for Johannesburg, one for Durban and one for Cape Town.

And an amazing thing happened.

By some strange coincidence all three trucks broke down on the way. Their refrigeration plants stopped functioning, their engines failed and it took some days for them to reach their markets.

All the meat was condemned as unfit for human consumption.

The scheme was abandoned. The farmers suffered a huge financial loss, the fat moneymakers smiled slyly behind their polished city desks and the city customers continued to eat a rather poor substitute for the real thing.

So, when you next visit the Karoo and are offered a helping of real Karoo mutton, please don't accept it. You'll never eat supermarket meat again.

For many years Jinna Ntame was our cook and I must confess she spoiled us rotten. Completely unflappable, she produced superb meals day after day, whether they were for two people or twenty. When unexpected guests arrived a few minutes before lunchtime, Mom would pop her head round the kitchen door and say: "There will be eight people for lunch today, Jinna."

And Jinna would say: "Yass, miesies," as calmly as ever and the meal would be ready when we arrived at the table half an hour later.

She usually had a whole leg or shoulder in the oven anyway so, whether it was to be eaten at one sitting or several, it was ready for us.

Her secret for producing perfect mutton every time was to cook it at low heat and very slowly. She used the real mutton, so she didn't need to add all the herbs and flavouring I've suggested. My modified version is meant to suit city-bought meat, and I offer it here, just in case you'd like a hint of what you're missing.

Jinna's lamb recipe

shoulder of lamb, deboned
1 handful of fresh breadcrumbs
1 handful of seedless raisins
1 heaped dessertspoon of fresh rosemary, finely chopped
1 teaspoon crushed garlic
½ cup sweet muscadel wine

Make a stuffing by mixing the breadcrumbs, raisins, rosemary and garlic together. Open the shoulder and spread them over it. Roll the meat up tightly with the stuffing inside and secure it with kitchen string. Place it in a large roasting pan, splash the muscadel wine over it, cover it with heavy duty foil and bake it at 110°C all afternoon if it is for dinner, or all morning if for lunch.
Bon appétit.

Oh, and don't let the rest of that bottle go to waste.

One Man and His Dog
Went to Mow a Meadow

The sheepdog, usually a Border collie, is an essential part of every Karoo farm's working team. The relationship between sheepdog and owner is quite different from the bond between a city human and a pet. There's no sentimental, kissy-face "Give daddy a big hug" nonsense about a proper sheepdog, but the bond between a farmer and his dog is probably closer than anything a city dog owner ever achieves.

This is a working partnership, not a love affair.

One interesting difference between sheepdogs and other fancy breeds is that there are no "beauty competitions" for sheepdogs. Looks simply don't count. They are judged solely on their ability to work efficiently with sheep.

Dog breeders begin their assessment of young dogs almost from birth, when every movement is observed and noted. Some pups are shy and allow themselves to be pushed aside by their siblings. Others are aggressive, but clumsy. Some will try to cross a ditch to reach a toy, and fall in. Others will figure out a way round. Slowly the breeder learns which of the litter has the most potential. These highly intelligent puppies are usually consigned to top handlers for training.

Anybody who gets a chance to do so should attend a sheepdog trial at least once. It's a fascinating experience. The usual test begins with a group of five sheep being released about a hundred metres away from the starting point, where the handler and his dog are waiting next to a small corral.

At the starting signal the handler sends the dog in a wide sweep to round up the sheep and bring them steadily toward the corral and in through the gate. The clock is stopped once all the sheep are inside and the handler closes the gate.

Sounds easy?

For one thing, a group of five sheep does not behave like a large flock. They tend to scatter in all directions, particularly in the unfamiliar surroundings of a showground, with noisy spectators and their dogs standing all around and making distracting noises. The dog must be fast and calm to gather all five, keep them together and obey his handler's commands.

I saw one young competitor lose his head completely and begin chasing a single sheep frantically around the grounds, ignoring the rest, which simply faded into the nearby car park or ambled off and began to graze on the nearby gardens. Eventually the panicked sheep saw the open door of a spectator's car and leapt in, cowering under the dashboard, much to the discomfort of the occupants.

Commands are given by whistles or hand signals or verbally.

There are set orders for "turn left" and "turn right"; commands for "come towards me" and "go away from me". Each dog handler develops his or her own set of commands.

"Bring 'em."

"Push 'em."

"A-waaay!"

"Come by."

Often the dog is out of sight of the farmer – and the sheep. This may be because of a rise in the terrain or long grass. Here the dog simply has to obey orders blind, relying on the fact that the farmer is high enough to see what is happening. You'll see that most Border collies have a white tip to their tails. This is considered a good feature, as it keeps the dog visible when it is otherwise hidden in long grass.

One of the best known of all South African sheepdog breeders and trainers was the legendary Ron Philip of Bredasdorp. You'll find farmers all over the country bragging quietly: "Jessie's father was bred by Ron Philip." It's the rural equivalent of the Sea Point boast: "My son is a doctor in Harley Street."

There's a much-told story about Ron Philip travelling to London to visit his daughter. When he arrived at Heathrow Airport it was, as always, packed from wall to wall with thousands of jostling, shoving, rude travellers, all trying to get somewhere else with their stacks of luggage. He was simply swept along willy-nilly, with no chance of finding his daughter.

With good sense she climbed a small flight of stairs and looked down for her father from the landing above the crowd. When she spotted him he was too far away to call him. Her dog-training background swung into play and she gave the shrill "this way" whistled command. Ron heard it and turned toward the sound, still not knowing where she was. She kept whistling dog commands – turn left, turn right – until he was almost directly under her and saw her.

Sometimes it's a good thing for the boss to learn the work of his staff.

In the days when all sheep work was done on horseback the dogs had to trot alongside, sometimes covering long distances before getting to where the sheep were. This necessitated long rest periods for the dogs' paws to recover after a strenuous session of sheep work.

Today on most farms off-road motorcycles have replaced horses. They don't have to be rounded up each morning, don't kick and they're faster and less trouble. Sheepdogs learn very quickly to jump up and ride on the pillion to get to work. It's much kinder to the paws. On our farm each motorcycle is fitted with a small tray on which one – or sometimes two – dogs balance as the machine bounces along the rutted farm tracks. It's a treat to see the dogs leaning this way and that as the bike takes the many corners. They grow to love motorcycling and come running to hop aboard as soon as they hear the engine starting.

Some years ago, when one of our shepherds, October Maliti, decided he was too old to ride a horse, he took to travelling to the camps on his balloon-tyred bicycle, with his faithful dog trotting quietly along behind him. At the camp gate he would stop, lean his bicycle against the gatepost and whistle the dog into action.

Soon all the sheep would be gathered, and October would mount his bicycle and start pedalling homeward without a backward look, knowing that the dog was bringing the flock along behind him.

Eventually the dog became too old and frail to accompany him to the veld, but the sheep – never the brightest of animals – didn't notice its absence.

October would arrive at the gate and open it, giving the usual whistled command, and the sheep would instinctively come running towards him. He would then pedal home and the flock would follow obediently, obviously convinced there was a dog behind them as always.

It caused much comment in the district. Most shepherds drove their flocks from behind. October led his from the front.

At one time there were several young learner farmers in the district and they all used to bring their sheepdogs along when they gathered at our farm for tennis on Saturday afternoons.

There's a sound reason for this, as sheepdogs become bored when they have no work to do and tend to trot off on their own and round up any sheep they can find, sometimes herding the flock hither and thither until the poor sheep almost collapse from exhaustion.

So they travel wherever the boss goes, or have to be shut up in a locked pen.

I remember one occasion when I watched in awe as the men organised an impromptu competition among themselves.

A lone chicken had come strutting across the lawn and one of the lads issued a challenge: "I bet I can get Jet to herd the chicken into that bucket."

The bucket was laid on its side and one by one the dogs rounded the chicken up and steered it, clucking indignantly, towards the bucket. By the time it was the last dog's turn to be tested, the chicken had had enough. It simply settled down in the bucket and refused to move out. The contest was declared a draw.

One thing most sheepdogs have in common is a fear of thunder.

Summer is the season of thunderstorms, and a Karoo thunderstorm is an impressive display, with great bolts of lightning hissing between the earth and heavy black clouds, to the accompaniment of crashes and rumbles of thunder.

It's all just too much for even the feistiest sheepdog and they usually come running indoors and spend the storm well hidden under the nearest bed.

The electric storms can also play havoc with electronics, not to mention regular power failures caused by lightning strikes on the Eskom grid.

Almost every Karoo farmer will tell you a story about his telephone exploding into fragments when lightning struck close by, or how the insides of the fax machine simply melted into a mess of copper and plastic. A smooth-talking salesman tried to sell my brother a special lightning arrester for the farm computer.

"It's not necessary," my brother said. "Long before the first lightning strikes us, we have already unplugged the computer and telephones."

"Ah, but how can you tell when lightning will strike?" he asked.

"No problem. Long before the storm starts the dogs have come inside and hidden under the beds. It's the best warning system there is."

Who would have thought the faithful Border collie would one day become an electronic early warning system?

Death in the Early Hours

Karoo farm children generally grow up with few illusions and very little squeamishness about life and death. Most farm kids have seen a sheep being slaughtered by the time they're able to walk. Out in the veld they will have come across animals that have died – either from sickness or being killed by predators.

It's just a normal part of life.

If an animal dies in the veld, its carcass lies in the hot sun until nature's scavengers – crows, vultures, ants, wildcats – come and clear it away. But before it is disposed of it sometimes blows up like a balloon as the stomach gases expand. Not a nice subject for the dinner table, maybe, but simply an accepted fact.

And when the deaths are caused by predators, like jackals or lynxes, they have to be destroyed. Once a predator develops a taste for Karoo lamb it can cause huge losses to the farmer. This sometimes means an organised hunt with the help of the neighbours.

One of our neighbours was Uncle Jack, a short, merry man with a large tummy and a permanent twinkle in his eye.

Uncle Jack used to watch the road through the spokes of his steering wheel, as he couldn't see over the top. Many out-of-town motorists had received rather a shock when they passed Uncle Jack's truck on the road and arrived at their destinations wide-eyed to report that they'd seen a runaway vehicle with no driver in it. He also used to place a napkin on his ample paunch when he drove, so the steering wheel didn't make a mark on his shirt.

Jackal hunts started before dawn, as the wily predators hunted at night and could sometimes be caught heading for their lairs at sunrise after a night's killing.

On one particular day the hunt was over, unsuccessfully, and the neighbours gathered round the host's truck for a cup of hot coffee from the thermos flask and a sturdy farm sandwich before setting off home.

For Uncle Jack it had been a very early start and the warm morning sun had lulled him to sleep at his post, so he missed the coffee and dozed peacefully.

After a while one of the hunters' little sons came running up to the group in excitement to announce: "Dad, there's a dead man over there behind the bushes. I think he must have been dead for a day or two because he's already blown up tight."

It was a story that Uncle Jack never lived down.

GOD MADE LITTLE GREEN APPLES AND LITTLE DIRTY BOYS

We were sitting under the shady vine that sheltered the stoep from the heat of the Karoo summer, my father and I, sipping a cold Castle and watching the mousebirds demolishing the hard little green apples that appeared every summer and never ripened into anything even vaguely tasty.

The giant apple tree had been there for as long as either of us could remember, producing its annual crop of tasteless little apples.

"Funny thing about those apples," said Dad. "I remember warning you kids every year not to eat green apples or you'd get sore tummies.

"I guess you all ate them anyway. Did you ever get a sore tummy from them?"

"Never," I said. "Not even a twinge."

"That's what's so strange," he said. "When we were children my father warned us every year that if we ate those green apples we'd get upset tummies. We ate them every summer and none of us ever had sore tummies."

I remembered quite clearly warning my own children that if they ate those green apples they'd get tummy-aches. A few days later I heard my son, Richard, warning his son, Henry, not to eat the green apples. That's five generations of warnings and never a single tummy-ache to justify them. Where do these unchanging rules of life originate? Perhaps it all started when Adam received his orders not to eat of the fruit of that tree in Eden. It didn't stop him either.

"Don't wave that stick around. You'll poke someone's eye out."

"Don't run with those scissors. You'll fall and cut yourself."

I must have heard them a hundred times and never heard of a single eye being poked out or a small runner being cut by scissors.

Generations of small children heard the warnings, ignored them and managed to survive long enough to warn their own children so they, in turn, could ignore them. I find it rather sad that so much of childhood is strictly regulated in these frightened times. I can only feel sorry for city children.

Young lives are wrapped in rules and regulations that almost make real play impossible. Playgrounds are shut down because the equipment does not comply with international standards. Toys are designed to be washable and have no sharp edges. Everything within metres of the growing child is sterilised, sanitised and wrapped in soft fuzz. Playhouses are neatly supplied in colourful non-toxic plastic. Surely this is not what growing up is all about.

My childhood on the farm was probably typical of the way most Karoo kids grew up. We were a gang of small ruffians – the twins Thumbi and Qayana, and Zwele, Tonose, Tiki and me. We enjoyed the free run of the farm and came home only when the sun set or hunger drove us indoors to the dining table.

Our parents never seemed to worry about where we were. They were probably as busy as we were and pleased to have us out of their way.

There never seemed to be enough hours in the day for all the things that needed doing. We were builders and hunters and sailors and warriors.

There was always plenty of raw material on the farm. Piles of used bricks could be turned into fine houses, and rusty corrugated iron sheets laid over the top to provide a roof, held down with assorted chunks of metal from the scrap yard. Every house needed a fireplace, so we set up a few stones and lit a dung fire between them and crowded into the tiny space until the acrid smoke caused tears to stream down our dirty little cheeks.

Chimneys were an unnecessary luxury and far too complicated to build.

We hunted dassies and birds with the inborn cruelty of small boys and "cooked" them over our smoky fires, and then ate them almost raw (who could wait until the meat was cooked right through?), assuring each other that it was delicious. There were prickly pears to be picked and peeled after rubbing them on the ground to remove the tiny thorns. A quince hedge provided the bitter fruit we pretended to enjoy after rubbing off the tough skins on a convenient rock. None of us ever seemed to suffer from this primitive diet.

We used old roofing sheets to build fine canoes, hammering out the corrugations on the concrete floor of the tractor shed, folding the metal up at the ends and sealing any holes with tar scraped off old discarded batteries.

The canoes floated well, but once they sank they stayed sunk. For small boys with skinny arms, no amount of lifting could retrieve a sunken tin canoe from the muddy bottom of the dam. We simply left them where they were and built another one. Nobody ever thought of building in any form of buoyancy.

Farm dams all over the Karoo must be a mine of corrugated iron from many sunken wrecks that have disappeared under the mud.

Maybe archaeologists will discover them in the far distant future and form intriguing theories about the prehistoric race of obviously very small sailors who launched fleets of iron ships in the sands of the Karoo.

Our battles were fought using the conveniently-shaped horse droppings as ammunition. A dried horse dropping has good aero-dynamics for accurate throwing, and is light enough not to cause serious injury.

A wet horse dropping was considered unsporting and probably banned by the Geneva Convention, unless the fight was a particularly acrimonious one. There is no revenge in the world sweet enough to compensate for the horrible feeling of being hit on the back of the head by a soggy wet horse dropping.

After the worst of these battles, my nanny Toen would insist that I change out of all my clothes before being allowed into the house to be scrubbed.

Of course there were accidents. We fell out of trees, we burned our hands and scraped our knees, or cut ourselves on the many sharp edges that exist in the real world. But we always survived. A dab of iodine stung like blazes, but seemed to prevent infection. A sticky plaster lasted a day or so before being scraped off in another adventure.

Interestingly none of us ever developed allergies. Our small bodies were probably so full of microbes, germs and assorted ingrained dirt that there simply wasn't room for new infections.

Maybe if we allowed children the freedom to enjoy a little dirt and danger there'd be less need for antibiotics and antihistamines in the modern world.

THIS IS THE RAT THAT ATE THE MALT THAT LAY IN THE HOUSE THAT JACK BUILT

Not a great deal happened in the old Albert Co-op in Middelburg. It's changed its name several times since I knew it, but it's still "the co-op".

Farmers occasionally drove in with their bakkies to load a few bags of laying mash or fill a gas cylinder or maybe buy a few cylinder leathers for the farm windmills. Mostly the staff sat and chatted and were pleased when a farmer popped in with news from the district.

But apparently a great deal went on in the storage shed at the back of the co-op after dark.

Mice.

Mice ate holes in the grain bags and the precious maize poured out onto the floor. They nibbled the pig-meal and munched the maize.

The co-op mice disdained the many traps that were set for them. After all, why should they bother with a piece of stale cheese when there was a mountain of good fresh grain for the taking?

The co-op manager imported a cat and turned her loose in the grain store. Each morning the cat would be found, totally bloated with mice. She lay on the grain bags burping faintly after a night of mouse gourmandising. She didn't want to look another mouse in the face.

And, in spite of the cat's nightly meals, the mouse population flourished and increased.

The co-op manager was at his wits' end.

Eventually a barefoot young schoolboy heard of the problem and wandered into the manager's office.

"I can solve your mouse problem," he announced, rather like the legendary Pied Piper of Hamelin Town.

The manager in desperation agreed to pay a bounty on every mouse destroyed, and the small boy smiled happily and took a large white rat from his blazer pocket, set it down in the grain store and, after giving the rodent an encouraging pat on the head, went about his daily business.

When the co-op manager opened his office the next morning, there was a neat row of a dozen dead mice. Each one had been bitten cleanly behind the head and set out on the floor for inspection.

This happened every day for a week, after which there were no more mice laid out for counting.

The small boy appeared at the office door once more, whistled for his white rat, pocketed it and his bounty and set off into the dusty streets to do the mysterious things that small boys do in country towns.

PASS, FRIEND

Looking back on it now, I realise that ours was an extraordinary childhood in an extraordinary era. At the time, of course, it seemed perfectly normal, because that was all we knew, being too young and too far removed from mainsteam politics even to have heard of apartheid and all its evil ramifications.

We white farm children grew up spending our busy days playing, squabbling, hunting, swimming and generally enjoying life with the children of the black farm labourers. Most of use learned to speak Xhosa quite naturally. It was the language of childhood. To this day, some fifty years later, my brother and sister and I often slip into Xhosa when we chat. It's a delightfully descriptive language. (My sister, who now lives in America, is sometimes irritated when she hears black Americans refer to themselves as "African Americans". "I am an African American," she says proudly. "You've never been to Africa and can't even speak an African language, but you have the cheek to call yourselves African!")

Inevitably the time came when we had to start school, and our lives parted ways. In our day – the 1940s and '50s – most English-speaking farmers' children went away to boarding school. Local schools were very Afrikaans and often biased against the English, probably a leftover from the South African War.

If the black kids were lucky, there was a rudimentary farm school near enough for them to attend where they generally learned little more than how to read and write. Few of the black schools went further than junior school level.

It was not very different when my father Norman was a lad, growing up on the farm Glenelg in the Steynsburg district. He once wrote to me describing his boyhood experiences.

"With our little black friends we played hide and seek, we fought great battles using dry horse dung and donkey droppings as ammunition. We used old sheets of corrugated roofing iron as sleds to slide down the high manure heaps until we smelled so bad that our mother used to order us to strip off all our clothing outside, before we were allowed to enter the house.

"There were deep kloofs to explore, birds' nests to discover, horses to ride and goats to try and inspan to little carts. Life was full and busy.

"But then tragedy struck. Suddenly we were old enough to start school and a governess arrived on the farm to give us lessons. We were confined to a schoolroom for five long, miserable hours every day when the whole exciting world outside was beckoning to us, and our little black playmates went on playing and laughing outside in the sunshine.

"Oh, woe were we! The unimaginable cruelty of big people!"

Then there were the infamous Pass Laws that restricted the movement of black people. They took an even stranger turn in country areas. If an African farm worker wanted to travel to town, or to any area not specified on his or her pass book, it was necessary to have a special written pass from a white person.

Any white person.

The crazy situation meant that I, as a little twelve-year-old white pip-squeak, could grant the necessary permission for a forty-year-old wage-earning black father of six children to travel the forty kilometres to town.

I remember many occasions when one of the workers would come and ask me to write a pass for him to take a goat or chicken to a relative in Noupoort.

"Please pass the bearer, Menziwe Ntame, to Noupoort with one goat. Signed David Biggs." All in a childish schoolboy handwriting. But a *white* schoolboy, so that made it legal.

We can only look back in some embarrassment.

Donkey Days

Every small boy needs transport. Today almost every city child starts with one of those ubiquitous black plastic motorbikes that roll about and seem to last forever, irritating parents and neighbours with their distinctive rumble. Later there are skateboards, scooters, roller blades and bicycles in that seemingly endless period of life before the first motorbike.

Things are rather different on a farm. My first vehicle was a donkey cart. I don't know where Dad found the donkey, Tony. In the misty clouds of memory, Tony was simply there one day and Longlegs (Ndoyisile Maliti) was sitting at the workbench stitching a harness for the little donkey.

Ndoyisile was an experienced harness-maker as he owned a fine team of mules, and could be seen every Saturday afternoon, setting off on his mule wagon with his wife Jane proudly seated beside him and his children piled on the back, off to do his social rounds.

Not only was Ndoyisile a good stockman and driver, he also performed the circumcisions when young Xhosa men reached the age for their traditional initiation. This gave him considerable status in the eyes of the community.

After his retirement, Ndoyisile told me proudly that he had circumcised more than a hundred boys and never had a health problem with one of them.

In due course the harness was ready and a reluctant Tony was pushed and pulled between the shafts of a little cart that was to be our little gang's transport for the next few years.

Anybody who has owned a donkey for any length of time will know that they were sent into the world to teach humans patience and humility. Most of our time with the donkey and cart was spent in almost tearful frustration, trying to untangle the donkey's back legs from the harness, or urging him in vain to go forward, or to stop.

My first team of donkey drivers and passengers consisted of children of farm staff. There were the usual gang – the twins, Thumbi and Qayana, Zwele, Tonose and the always-naughty Tiki.

Xhosa was our language as we tumbled from adventure to adventure across the farm. I have always been grateful that I grew up speaking Xhosa, as it is not an easy language for an English tongue to learn from scratch later in life.

From the front of the shed the road sloped gently downward to the corner, where there was a sharp bend to the left.

An average start to a ride on the donkey cart began with Tony setting off downhill like a rocket, being helped along by the weight of the cart (which had no brakes) and its small passengers. By the time the speeding vehicle reached the bend we had achieved quite a turn of speed – usually too fast to take the corner – and the whole lot would crash sickeningly into the fence.

The two shafts of the cart would stick through the wire and the cart would continue forward, compressing the donkey considerably. Tony would then kick in anger (understandably) and get one or both back legs hooked up on to the bed of the cart.

Deadlock.

Everybody climbed off the cart and surveyed the problem, all offering useful advice at top volume. The first thing was to get Tony's back feet off the cart, but this could not happen until the cart had been pulled back a bit, to uncrumple the unfortunate squeezed donkey. This was complicated by the fact that the shafts had become stuck in the fence, so they had to be untangled first.

The danger here was that Tony was an angry beast by now and ready to bite anybody who approached within snapping range. Eventually, accompanied by many shouts and smacks, the whole cavalcade would be reassembled and pointed in the general direction of the road.

Theoretically we were now set to roll.

Often Tony had ideas of his own and simply refused to budge another step. After an hour or so of pushing and pulling we would come to the end of our attention spans, unhitch the donkey and push the cart back uphill into the shed.

I sometimes wonder why we bothered.

But there are memories of wonderful rides, too, when the little donkey trotted swiftly along the dusty road and we lay on our backs in the cart, chatting lazily and watching the clouds drift by and the crows circling high overhead. We visited neighbouring farms and were treated to biscuits and lemon syrup before setting off for home, full and happy.

Oh, the freedom of the open road!

Tony was never reluctant for the homeward journey. The last few kilometres were always achieved at breakneck speed. He knew he'd be free to graze and dream – free of the pestiferous little swarm of noisy boys – once he reached the peace of the farmyard.

All good things come to an end, though, and I was eventually sent away to boarding school and Tony was retired to pasture in the lush part of the farm known as the Vlei.

Some time later, however, he became bored with his retirement and took to biting the sheep, sometimes so severely that they died.

Obviously he had to go and was given to the local brick maker, Kolana Ntame, who had a brickyard in Noupoort. Tony ended his days walking slowly in circles, operating the pug mill that kneaded the clay for Kolana's bricks. It was certainly a more peaceful career than transporting hordes of noisy children.

Tears on the Platform

Today Noupoort station is a forlorn place. The long concrete platform is cracked and weeds sprout everywhere. Many of the railway buildings are empty and their windows broken. Dry tumbleweeds roll along between the rusty lines when the west wind blows. In what was once the busy passenger subway, vagrants have set up their ragged homes. The few trains that pass through seldom stop here and, if they do, it is only for a few moments before setting off for more prosperous places like Johannesburg, Cape Town or Port Elizabeth.

Whole streets of railway houses have been torn down, leaving weed-strewn gravel where large families once lived. Even now, when it all seems abandoned and neglected, the sight of the Noupoort station raises a little lump of nostalgic fear, loneliness and sadness in my throat. For ten long years, three times a year, I spent dismal evenings on that platform waiting for the 9.30 pm train that would take me overnight to boarding school in Grahamstown. It was a busy, bustling place in those days. I believe more than a hundred trains used to pass through Noupoort every day at the peak of its operation. Today there are only one or two.

We would stand together on the platform, a small group of four or five children and their parents, waiting for the school train, wanting the farewell to be over quickly and at the same time dreading the train's arrival.

There was big Stan Bennett, tall George de Jager, the Southey boys, myself, and later my brother Roger and sister Daphne, usually huddled in corners sheltered from the icy wind that always seemed to blow in Noupoort on school train days.

Our suitcases lined up in a neat row, together with the inevitable rug strap buckled round a tartan travelling rug, with a wooden Dunlop Maxply tennis racquet tucked in the centre and a shoebox of tuck for the journey. Not much was said. Our parents talked quietly together of farming things like the weather, the price of wool, the drought and the cost of power paraffin for the tractors. The kids stood forlornly and occasionally punched each other half-heartedly, in the universal small boys' form of communication.

Then the train would come roaring in, with a shriek of its whistle, the squeal of metal wheels on metal rails, a hiss of hot steam and the unforgettable smell of coal smoke, hot oil and hot polished metal. The conductor stepped down with his clipboard and parents lined up to get the number of their children's compartments. Often a stick of springbok biltong or two would change hands to ensure that a young passenger was put in a good compartment and well looked after.

Last minute messages from mothers: "Don't forget to write. I've put a little something in your case for you to open when the train leaves."

And fathers: "Now you keep practising that tennis serve, see? I want to see you serving all aces when you come home next holidays."

And the inevitable: "It's not a long term. You'll be home before you know it."

Lies. The terms were all eternally long.

But young people are incredibly resilient and it took only a few minutes after leaving the station for farm life to slip away and school manners and language to kick in. We'd be swopping comic books, comparing the contents of tuck-boxes and recounting the adventures of the holidays almost before the lights of Noupoort had disappeared into the night.

"Who do you think will be head of house this year?"

"Hope it's not Smith. He's a poephol."

"Is Gaydon coming back for post-matric? We could win the inter-house rugby if he does."

I was told later that it took our parents far longer to get rid of that sad, sour lump in the throat, and that the drive home, for them, was always a mournful affair with little talk.

There are, of course other memories of Noupoort – happier ones.

Mom (Clarice Biggs, née Rogers) was an enthusiastic breeder of fine, pedigreed Persian cats. There was always a waiting list for the Grapevale kittens and they were usually despatched to their new owners by train.

The train service was efficient and very reliable in those days, and the journey from Noupoort to Port Elizabeth – which is where most of the kittens went –

was a relatively short overnight trip. The kittens were sent in neat wooden crates with wire mesh tops, that had been carefully constructed by my father, Norman.

At first they tried putting containers of milk and cat food in the crates with the kittens, but this proved far too messy. Invariably the milk would be splashed out and the kitten would arrive sodden in sour milk and matted with mushed food.

It was decided that the little travellers could cope very well without food for the few hours of the overnight journey, and from then on they arrived in very good condition. Their new owners were always waiting to collect them when the train arrived at the other end.

The railway authorities, however, had very set ideas about the transport of livestock. Regulations were regulations.

"You can't send the cat like that," said one stationmaster. "Animals have to be given food for the journey."

My father was a patient man, who never raised his voice or displayed any bad temper. He had a quiet sense of humour that endeared him to everybody and usually carried him through any scrapes with the authorities. He saw it was hopeless to try to get the stationmaster to bend the rules in this case.

A little way from the station platform was a stack of bags of maize, one of which had a tear in the corner and some mielies had leaked out in a small pile.

Carefully Dad scooped up a handful of the dry maize kernels and poured them through the wire mesh.

"There," he said, "now the cat has food for the journey."

The stationmaster scratched his head.

"Cat's don't eat mielies," he said.

"Not most cats," Dad agreed quietly, "but our cats are raised on nothing else but mielies. It's all they eat."

After a long pause the consignment note was stamped and signed.

From then on all the Grapevale kittens set off on the train with a few mielies for *padkos*. They all arrived in fine condition and we often received letters telling us of the latest championships and trophies they had won at cat shows all over the country.

When the train services began to deteriorate it became too complicated to send cats to faraway destinations and Mom stopped breeding her Persians.

The last of the Grapevale Persian line died in 2003 at a great old age, in Denmark. But that's another story.

ALL CREATURES GREAT AND SMALL

Towards the end of the school term I was exploring the exciting clay quarry near the potteries outside Grahamstown with some pals. The quarry was technically out of bounds, but that never proved a deterrent to small boys. You could often find discarded pieces of pottery there – almost whole teapots and plates, or little vases shaped like Dutch clogs. It was a boys' treasure trove.

On this occasion we discovered something completely different – a baby owl had fallen from its nest high up on the quarry face and was flapping about pathetically among the pottery shards. It was very young and had not yet lost all of its baby pinfeathers. A sad sight indeed. Of course we gathered it up and I carried it back to boarding school in the front of my shirt, where it left its marks, which never disappeared in spite of frequent washing. Once back at school I placed the little chick in my suitcase and propped the lid open a crack for air.

Luckily (like most of the farm kids who spoke Xhosa) I was on good terms with the black kitchen staff and soon organised a regular supply of minced meat.

At first Horace (which was the name we selected for him, by committee) was reluctant to take the meat but, after having it forcibly stuffed into his gaping beak once or twice, he got the message and became a complete glutton, tottering about with his huge beak gaping wide every time anybody approached the suitcase. In the two weeks before the term ended Horace almost doubled in size.

He accompanied me home on the train in a cardboard box and was accepted without too much fuss by my ever-patient parents. (Although my mother did seem rather put out by the state of the inside of my suitcase. I hadn't thought it necessary to put down any sort of lining.)

Horace took up residence on the dressing table in my bedroom, with a good supply of old newspapers under him. Here he dozed the days away, waking every evening with a great snapping of his beak demanding to be fed.

Food was never a problem on the farm, as there were mice to be caught in the storeroom and marauding mousebirds to be shot in the apple trees.

Soon Horace was big enough to take his first hesitant flight from the bedroom window, out over the garden and back, obviously rather pleased with himself.

By the time the long summer holidays drew to a close Horace was almost completely independent, still sleeping on the dressing table all day, but taking off on his nightly hunts, usually returning with a mouse held firmly in his beak. He would swallow it whole, working it into his throat in convulsive jerks, a process that took several minutes and was truly disgusting to watch. Eventually only the tail would be left dangling from the corner of his beak and he would close his eyes and appear to doze off for half an hour or so with the tail hanging out like half a Chinese mandarin's moustache.

Later Horace found a mate and tried in vain to persuade her to come home and meet the family. She refused, and the two sat forlornly in the branches of the pine tree outside my bedroom, with him pleading, in hoots and clicks, for her to come with him. The female of every species, however, is a hard-hearted creature, and Horace eventually had to choose between her and us. Inevitably love won the contest and he flew off with his lady to start a family.

For some years later, whenever we saw a spotted eagle owl we'd wonder whether it could be one of Horace's descendants. I often wondered whether he ever thought back fondly of his old perch on the dressing table. I hope so.

The Karoo is home to a vast variety of small animals and birds and it was inevitable that we children would collect orphans of one kind or another over the years.

I still have a vivid memory of my father and mother doing their evening inspection stroll around the vegetable garden, followed by the pets in descending order of rank. My parents would lead the way closely followed by Beau, the fat corgi, then the Persian cats, Snickanoodle and Lilywoo, and finally, stepping sedately along, Shelley, the blue crane. It was a slow and very solemn procession.

Later we acquired Bonnie, a baby dassie. Bonnie moved in in winter and immediately took up the prime spot in front of the evening fire, snuggling down among the cats and stretching out to get the full warmth of the flames on his tummy. After a while he would become uncomfortably hot and roll over to toast his back for a bit, usually shoving a peeved cat out of the way as he did so. My mother was rather fond of Bonnie, and used to boast to visitors that he was the cleanest pet we'd ever had. He never made a single mess in the house, she said.

When spring arrived it was time for the great annual spring clean, a ritual the whole farm dreaded. The entire staff was involved: the furniture had to be dragged out into the garden, carpets taken out and shaken, walls cleaned, floors polished, books dusted and the whole lot put back in place. The big easy chairs were the first to be moved, then the couch. This proved a problem. Somehow the couch seemed to have stuck to the floor. After much pulling and hauling it was finally lifted, but needed four strong men to carry it outside.

Once in the garden the mystery was solved. All winter Bonnie had been using the inside of the couch as his toilet, packing layer upon layer of droppings among the springs and webbing until they formed a solid, rock-hard mound. There must have been almost a ton of manure in there. The remarkable thing was that it had no unpleasant smell. Or maybe we'd simply grown accustomed to it.

We bought a new couch and my mother watched Bonnie like a hawk after that. He had to spend time outside every evening. He never enjoyed that. Bonnie was strictly a house dassie.

Jerry the crow was a source of endless amusement to the family. Grapevale was always the centre of social activity in the district and every weekend of the summer holidays saw a crowd of young people gathered around the tennis court and swimming pool. And Jerry was always there too, hopping about among the guests and stealing anything shiny.

We eventually had to keep a ladder close at hand to retrieve watches, spectacles and cigarette lighters from the gutters, where Jerry had taken them. He enjoyed swiping a packet of cigarettes and flying up to the roof with them. There he would take them out one by one and shred them while the assembled party below shouted and threw cushions at him in an attempt to save some of the cigarettes.

Crows have telescopic eyesight and whenever Jerry wanted to know where any of the family was he would simply circle higher and higher until he was a mere speck in the sky. From there he would survey the whole farm, select a companion and glide down to settle on his or her shoulder with a friendly croak and tweak of the ear. This was all very well for those of us who knew Jerry, but it caused the abandonment of an important club match on one occasion.

The Tafelberg Tennis Club, the other side of Middelburg, were our strongest rivals. This match was on our courts (we were the Hantam Tennis Club) and the results were very even until Jerry, back at the house, must have realised that everybody had gone away.

As usual, he soared up to a great height and looked down. And there we all were, gathered at the tennis club about a kilometre away. Wings folded, Jerry dropped like a black rocket, just as an energetic Tafelberg lady was preparing to serve.

She threw the ball up, swung back her racquet... and froze. From high above her a small black speck was increasing rapidly in size and a large crow – bird of ill omen (just ask Edgar Alan Poe) – swooped down over her head and settled comfortably on the net in front of her. She shrieked in terror and fled the court, twisting her ankle painfully on the steps as she left.

The match ended in confusion and was declared a draw.

Quite recently my brother Roger shared his home with a family of meerkats who used to enjoy watching television. Roger and his wife Penny are keen followers of soap operas and it was an interesting sight to see them settled down on their couch, ready for the next episode of *Isidingo*, with the row of little meerkats sitting bolt upright in front of the screen, occasionally making little "uck-uck-uck" comments to each other, probably endlessly mystified by the strange goings-on of the human race. Who could blame them?

I suppose my very first pet was Penelope, a small pink piglet given to me when I was five years old. Pigs have had a very bad press and are usually associated with dirt and bad manners. In reality they're rather fastidious and well-mannered animals. Penelope could have fitted comfortably into a shoebox when she arrived, and shared my bed in a very friendly way. She followed me everywhere, trotting along behind me and snuffling her flat little nose into anything that appeared worth investigating.

Pigs grow up far quicker than small boys and by the time I was six Penelope was about twice my size and taking up far more than her share of the bed. At this stage my parents decided it was time for me to begin my education and I was sent off to the farm Hughdale, about twenty kilometres away, as a weekly border.

Hughdale belonged to Hugh and Marie Barnes-Webb, who had a daughter, Anne, exactly my age, and Aunt Marie turned out to be a natural teacher for little beginners. From her we learned our reading and writing, nature study and drawing and a million useful things I remember to this day.

Our classes were held in a rondavel in the yard and we addressed her as "Teacher" during classes. At midday we would stop lessons and go to the house for lunch, where Aunt Marie had always prepared a meal to delight small palates. And such was her magic that we would spend all lunchtime telling Aunt Marie what "Teacher" had taught us during the morning.

I would be taken to Hughdale early on Monday morning and return home on Friday afternoon or Saturday morning. Anne and I were as close as brother and sister and those first two years of school were a great joy. I suppose it was natural that Penelope should resent my long absences, and she began to show her irritation by nipping me hard whenever I arrived back home and claimed my room.

One fateful weekend she overstepped the mark and gave me quite a severe bite on the leg, resulting in floods of tears and some blood.

My parents must have decided it was time for the pig to go. Next weekend Penelope was no longer there. I looked around for her and asked what had happened to her. Dad said she had gone away to school, like me.

Mom said she was sure Penelope was happy where she was, and helped me to another slice of home-cooked ham.

PLAY UP AND PLAY THE GAME

Cricket has always featured large in my family, although I must confess I never enjoyed the game. My father was a selector for the Eastern Province Country Districts team and used to be invited to Port Elizabeth to watch the visiting overseas teams in action at St George's Park. This was a matter of some pride in the family, although it must have strained the budget to the limit. Cricket was a purely amateur sport in those days and all expenses were born by the participants.

Even Springbok cricketers were unpaid and had to find the money needed for overseas tours. They did it purely for the honour of representing their country.

My brother, Roger, played for the St Andrew's College first cricket team and my cousin, Anthony Biggs, known as "Dassie", was actually selected to play for the Springbok cricket team, but the tour was cancelled that year because of anti-apartheid sport boycotts.

My uncle Llewellyn, "Wellie" (Dassie's dad), was a devoted cricket player and, frankly, terrified me as a small boy as he always seemed to be throwing hard balls at me at unexpected moments. His right arm would swing overhead in a bowling action, cornering my concentration, and the ball would come sneaking out of his left hand, just at groin height. It always caught me squarely in the tummy, raising a hearty laugh from Uncle Wellie and making me feel a complete idiot. We shared a birthday, though, so I felt we had something in common, in spite of my constantly bruised belly button whenever he came to visit.

The highlight of the Colesberg cricket season was the Fathers versus Sons match played on the local showgrounds every year on December the 31st and followed that night by the New Year's Eve dance in the town hall.

The showgrounds were a rather dusty, dry place surrounded by stables and judging rings, all made of creosote poles and corrugated iron, and smelling of manure and stale straw and only slightly sheltered by tall blue-gum trees that shed a great number of leaves and provided little shade.

The horse stables served as changing rooms and toilets and the members' enclosure provided space for the cricketers' wives to brew tea on roaring Primus stoves and serve scones spread with melted butter to the players. There was no need to cater for spectators, as there weren't any, apart from the families of players.

I remember those matches as being long, achingly boring days, either standing out on the field in the baking sun for hours, waiting for something interesting to happen, or sitting in a parked car on the boundary waiting for my turn to bat.

This was usually at number 11 and never lasted more than an over. Somehow the Biggs cricket gene had passed me by.

I don't suppose there are many Karoo towns that can field a whole cricket team today, but the game obviously played an important role in the social life of the country during the last century.

When you're travelling northward on the great N1 highway, watch for a little cluster of tombstones and memorials to the right of the road, about twelve kilometres before the village of Matjiesfontein. Take a few minutes to navigate the bumpy little dirt road down to the cemetery and spend some time among those historic graves. One that always captures my imagination is the ornate grave of George Alfred Lohmann, whose headstone describes him as: "One of the greatest all-round cricketers the world has ever seen".

It states that Lohmann "… did brilliant service for Surrey from 1884 to 1896. Ill health alone compelled him to retire from the cricket field while still in his prime." Lohmann died in 1901 at the age of thirty-six.

He probably came to Matjiesfontein for health reasons, as the little town was founded as a place where patients suffering from respiratory diseases like consumption (tuberculosis) could recover in the healthy Karoo air.

But to me the most poignant part of this mighty cricketer's grave is a small white marble cross that lies at the foot of the impressive headstone.

The inscription reads: "In loving memory of George this cross is placed here by a faithful friend. Peace to him that is far off and to him that is near."

Who was the sorrowing anonymous friend so far off? An old school pal? A fellow team member? Did he mourn far away in Surrey after hearing the news of his friend's death? Was the little white cross made in a stonemason's workshop in Britain, to be shipped out and placed at the foot of Lohmann's grave?

The wide open spaces of the Karoo hold so many stories that will probably never be told.

Matjiesfontein, incidentally, claims to be the venue of the first ever international cricket match to be played in South Africa. It was between a local team and a visiting team that travelled from England. The photographs of that historic match can be seen in the Laird's Arms pub next to the Lord Milner Hotel.

My family's devotion to cricket, incidentally, caused me some fearful nightmares when, at the age of eight, I was being prepared for boarding school. At that stage I had absolutely no idea what to expect from this new adventure.

For several weeks my mother sorted piles of new school clothes, sewing endless nametapes to unfamiliar garments like ties (I'd never worn one), blazers and long grey socks. And the new tartan travelling rug with fringes and its own leather rug strap. I watched these preparations with some alarm, especially when I was told gently: "Now you just make sure you look after these clothes, see?"

I could not imagine what boarding school would be like and imagined myself dumped in the middle of the veld somewhere with my pile of clothes and having to guard them against unknown thieves.

Nobody thought to explain that there would be cupboards and lockers at boarding school. Or somebody to look after my clothes.

Then there was the matter of "rugby".

Since we were a strictly cricketing and tennis-playing family, rugby had never been mentioned in our home. I'd never seen or heard of rugby, but parents, uncles and aunts were suddenly discussing it above my head.

"Do you think he'll be starting rugby this year?"

"Probably not. It's a bit dangerous for such young kids."

"Oh, I don't know. They like to get them toughened up while they're very young these days."

Rugby? What could it mean? Obviously it had something to do with rugs – probably the new tartan rug and its leather strap. And it was dangerous. In my nightmares I was trapped under that rug while hordes of bigger boys stomped on me dangerously and tied me up with the leather strap to make me tough.

I sometimes wonder whether adults realise the torments they inflict on their children by a simple lack of explanation.

OF MOLES AND MEN

My father was a steady man, not given to sudden enthusiasm. Apart from his deep love of the land he enjoyed playing tennis and cricket and being surrounded by his family. His hobbies included woodworking and he left us with some fine sturdy furniture.

But on one occasion he broke out of the mould and decided – with a few of his friends – to take up bird shooting in the true English style. His main ally in the venture was the local attorney and auctioneer, Mr Jack Garlake, an impressive man of considerable girth and imposing presence. Jack and his wife Ella were close friends of my parents'. Together they bought a pair of enthusiastic pointer dogs, called Dainty and Fancy, polished up the old family 12-bore shotguns and planned a winter of weekend partridge shoots in the mountains.

I believe they saw themselves as country squires striding the moors of Scotland after grouse. And indeed they were an impressive sight, marching across the veld, dressed in hunting jackets, with bulky belts of number 7 cartridges slung round their waists, while Dainty and Fancy ranged to and fro ahead of them, sniffing every bush and tuft of *suurpol* grass.

Eat your heart out, Jock MacTaggert.

Occasionally one of the dogs would freeze in the typical pointer stance – one front foot raised, tail straight out behind, nose pointing at the bush or tussock where the quarry was hiding. The hunters would stop and tension would build up to an almost unbearable pitch until there was a sudden flurry of wings and a partridge would burst from cover and take off in a fast, low trajectory. Guns were raised and shots boomed out. The air filled with the heady smell of cordite.

This actually happened once or twice.

Usually what scampered from hiding was a hare or meerkat, or possibly a dassie. Rather an anticlimax. I don't believe a great number of partridges ever made it into partridge pie, but that was not the main object of the exercise.

It was really about camaraderie, handling fine guns, following excited dogs and enjoying a good walk in mountains in the bracing chill air of the Karoo winter. The evenings would be spent around the fire, cleaning the guns and discussing the day's shoot, the birds that had got away and the fine way the dogs had performed. The wives feigned interest and sipped their gins and tonics.

All very civilised.

There were setbacks, of course. On one occasion one of the hunters, who had finished refilling his cartridge belt, crumpled up the empty cardboard box and tossed it into the fire. Suddenly there was an ear-shattering bang and the fire simply vanished. The astonished hunters and their families regained their senses and opened their eyes to an unusual sight. Everybody was covered in white ash from head to foot, as was the lounge furniture.

Large eyes blinked nervously from white masks. You've heard the expression "ashen-faced"? Well.

In the silence a rather shaky voice said, "Sorry about that, chaps. Thought the box was empty."

Between shoots Dainty and Fancy tended to become bored and ranged about the yard, worrying the bantam hens and chasing each other's tails.

On one memorable occasion an unsuspecting mole popped up out of the lawn and crawled about in the grass until it was discovered by the dogs, who found it most interesting and both pointed at it enthusiastically.

Slowly, quivering with excitement, Dainty inched forward until her nose was just a few millimetres from the invader. The mole obviously didn't take kindly to the sudden waft of dog-breath, and turned angrily and attached itself firmly to Dainty's nose.

With a scream of pain, the dog tore off, with the unfortunate mole swinging from her snout. Right round the house she ran, yelping and howling, and trying for all she was worth to shake off the nasty painful thing that was attached to her nose.

Eventually the mole let go and had just begun to return underground when Fancy came trotting up, rather puzzled, to see what had caused all the fuss.

This was more than enough for the now furious rodent. It gave one savage lurch (moles don't "pounce", as a rule) and attached itself to a new nose. Fancy now understood the problem all too clearly and simply sat and howled, shaking his head vigorously until the mole dropped off.

Both dogs then retreated to a safe spot to lick their wounds and regain their dignity while the mole busily buried itself once more in the safety of the earth.

After the disappearance of Dainty and Fancy (I have no idea where they went; they may have been sold while I was away at school), Dad was offered a bird dog pup with a great pedigree and an impossibly aristocratic name, which nobody ever remembered. It was a clumsy puppy, constantly falling over its own feet in its efforts to be friendly.

It became known as Hunky-tunk – a suitably undignified name. This lanky dog, a Gordon setter, came recommended as the perfect breed of bird dog and probably cost a fortune. It would be ready for training in good time for next winter's shooting season, we were assured.

Hunky-tunk grew, but didn't mature very well. He continued to trip over things and grin foolishly when it happened.

Eventually it was time to begin his training and we set off on a walk in the veld, carrying shotguns. The very first thing a gun dog must learn, obviously, is not to be afraid of guns. The sporting world has no place for a gun-shy dog.

Hunky-tunk ranged about ahead of us enthusiastically, enjoying the walk, until a partridge suddenly burst out of a tuft of long grass and took off in a flurry of wings. Hunky-tunk screamed in fright, turned tail and headed for home as fast as his unco-ordinated feet would carry him. He tripped several times before he was out of sight and we found him later, cowering under the sofa and whimpering.

No shots had been fired.

Dad gave up in disgust and gave Hunky-tunk to a friend in town. It was embarrassing enough to own a gun-shy gun dog, but a bird-shy bird dog was something nobody could ever live down.

The shooting passion had cooled and the guns were oiled and packed away neatly in their leather cases. Occasionally they are taken out and admired. The engraving on the barrels is very fine.

BABOONS AND BALL VALVES

Every farmer will agree: baboons are pests. The rocky Karoo koppies make ideal hiding places for the large troops of baboons that range over many kilometres of territory, undeterred by boundary fences and facing very little opposition. Once there were leopards in the mountains to keep the baboon population in check. Today their only enemy is man. The two traits that contribute to the universal unpopularity of the baboons are their endless curiosity and their cleverness.

When a baboon discovers a water tap or a grain silo or a box of tools, he simply has to take it apart to see what is inside. Their agile fingers are incredibly strong from years of lifting stones to find insects and grubs underneath.

Kenilworth, the farm next to ours, had been owned by the Howes family until my Uncle Neville's death at the end of the war, when Aunt Elma sold it to my father. Nobody lived at the farmhouse after this. Most of the main building was dismantled and the doors, roof and windows salvaged for use in other farm buildings. A shed and storeroom were retained and kept securely locked.

In the shed were two large galvanised iron tanks used for storing grain.

The abandoned farmstead proved just too much of a temptation to the local baboon population. They picked away at doors and window frames, eventually breaking the glass panes and biting through the wooden frames. Once inside, they explored the grain tanks, picking and scratching and pulling until they had made holes, from which the grain spilled onto the floor.

Outside there were rows of spineless prickly pear trees, planted as emergency stock feed for dry years. Every summer they produced large, sweet red fruit, which the baboons loved. Unfortunately the fruit caused the baboons to produce bright purple droppings, which they deposited all over the ruptured grain tanks and surrounding floor. It was a total mess.

Shooting them was not a great solution. One or two might be killed and the rest would vanish into the hills until the danger was over, and then return to continue their destruction, wiser and wilier than before.

There were more of them than there were of us.

Pretty soon they learned to distinguish between a man (who might be concealing a gun) and a woman, who was generally harmless. The baboons became so bold that they wandered freely among the Xhosa women who came to the old homestead to "*theza*", or collect firewood.

When the women arrived the baboons took no notice of them at all.

Eventually October Maliti, the chief sheep-man, suggested that he dress up as a woman and conceal a shotgun under his skirt. The plan worked perfectly and October strolled right into the marauding troop before pulling out the gun and scaring the living daylights out of the baboons, which scattered in panic, leaving bright purple trails along the path as they fled. After that they continued as destructive as ever, but always stayed away when humans of either sex appeared.

Always looking for new solutions to the problem, Dad set a cage trap baited with mielies and caught a large male baboon in it. He then proceeded to spray the baboon from head to toe with white house paint, using a stirrup pump, and released it. The ghostly white baboon scampered off to his family and we didn't see them for a few months.

Apparently the painted male approached the troop, expecting to be welcomed home. But the family saw this dreadful white apparition coming toward them

and fled. The white baboon must have wondered what they were running from, and joined the retreat. And so they fled until they were far from the farm. I suppose the rain or sweat must eventually have cleaned the paint from the baboon. In due course they were back, of course, but we had enjoyed a few peaceful baboon-free weeks.

Among their favourite targets for destruction were the plastic balls that operated the valves in the sheep water troughs. Water is a precious commodity in the Karoo and care is taken not to waste a drop. Ball valves are fitted to the troughs so they're kept full of drinking water, but don't overflow. As the water level drops, the valve opens and allows more water in.

The bright plastic floats were simply irresistible to the inquisitive baboons.

They would remove the heavy stone covering the valve, then tug and twist and pull on the plastic ball, worrying it until it broke off, after which they'd chew it to shreds while the trough filled, overflowed and eventually drained all the precious water from the supply reservoir, creating a muddy swamp around the trough.

On one of his shopping trips to Middelburg my father stopped at the co-op and asked for half a dozen new plastic balls.

"Why do you use so many of them?" asked the co-op salesman.

"Because the baboons break them as fast as I can replace them," muttered Dad.

"Oom Norman," said the salesman, "I notice that the farmers in the mountain areas, where there are lots of baboons, buy green ball valves, rather than orange ones. They say the baboons don't bother so much with green valves."

Well, Dad was happy to try anything that might work, so the troughs were duly fitted with green plastic balls and to everybody's surprise the baboon destruction ceased. The next time he was in the co-op, Dad thanked the man for his suggestion and wondered idly why baboons pulled out the orange valves but left the green ones.

"Oh, that's quite simple," said the salesman. "The baboons think the green ones are not ripe yet."

Hark, Hark,
the Dogs Do Bark

One of the most exciting events in my childhood was the annual visit of the circus – Boswell's or Pagel's – to Noupoort. Weeks before the time the town would be papered with brightly coloured posters announcing the dates. You could feel the excitement rising. On the farm, forty kilometres from Noupoort, word would soon arrive that the circus was coming to town. Would we be allowed to go?

"Well," Dad would say, "it all depends on how much work we get done by then. We still have to dip all those sheep up in the mountain camp before the bont-leg ticks start worrying them. Times are tough and we need to save all the money we can. We'll just have to see whether we can afford the circus this year."

The anticipation would build up unbearably.

And of course Dad always relented, as we knew he would.

The farm staff would be gathered together for the announcement.

"You chaps can knock off work tomorrow at lunchtime and take the tractor and trailer to Noupoort to see the circus. You must stop at the spruit just outside the town and wait for us to meet you there."

The tractor, an ancient "Bluebottle" Fordson, had a top speed of about twenty kilometres per hour, so it would take the staff at least two hours to reach town. The family would set off later in the truck. In the late afternoon family and staff would meet in the dry riverbed outside the town for a picnic. Then the whole cavalcade would rumble into Noupoort.

Nothing can compare with the noise, sights and smells of the old-fashioned circus. A great diesel generator roared in the background providing electricity for the strings of bright lights suspended over the vast circus tent. Lions growled in their wheeled cages, elephants trumpeted and the reedy sound of the steam organ wafted its tinny music across the circus ground. The air was filled with the pungent odour of lion pee and elephant droppings. Busy workers hammered tent stakes in more firmly, rigging was tightened and checked, and gaggles of children watched as caravans were moved into position. Jugglers and tumblers practised their acts quietly behind their mobile homes.

In the Biggs camp heads were counted – so many black children, so many black adults, so many white adults and so many white children. There were different ticket prices for each category. Tickets were purchased and handed out and the crowd surged into the tent to grab good seats. Black and coloured spectators sat on one side, whites on the other. And the show began. We gasped at the daring trapeze artists, marvelled at the bareback riders and gaped at the elephants, ponderously rising up to stand on their hind feet.

Performers juggled with flaming torches, swallowed swords and rode bicycles along tight wires. There was a sense of danger in every act, and it kept us all on the very edges of our seats. But it was the clowns that captured our hearts. We howled with laughter, we giggled and shrieked at their antics. Tickey the Clown

and his friends came tumbling and shouting into the ring between acts and played directly to the black and coloured gallery – and they loved every moment.

For weeks afterwards the farm work would suddenly stop as somebody remembered a particularly funny incident. The animal acts were forgotten. The acrobats and trapeze fliers were a mere faded memory. But every moment of the clown acts stayed in our minds as vividly as if it were five minutes ago.

"Man, did you see when Tickey squirted water into the other one's ear and his hat flew off!"

And there'd be fresh gales of mirth.

"Remember how his trousers fell down when the car exploded?"

More chuckles and an energetic mime of that particular part of the act and we'd all end up wiping tears of happy laughter from our eyes yet again. Jislaaik, it was funny! We'd all seen every act when we were there, but we told each other the details over and over, simply for the joy of re-living those magical moments.

The old Roman emperors had a good point when they decreed that the people should be given bread and circuses. I suspect that a couple of clowns do more good for the souls of the nation than all the politicians in parliament.

On the other hand, isn't that what we have?

FROM BLUE TO BICYCLES

When I was a lad the highlight of any trip to Middelburg was a visit to Mr Nicholas's bicycle shop. For a small boy it was a cave of wonders. Bicycle frames hung from the ceiling alongside festoons of tyres of all sizes. Boxes of bicycle bells were stacked side-by-side with pumps, spokes, tins of ball bearings, torches, screws, washers, nuts, bolts, oilcans, Primus stove spares and all kinds of handy tools.

David Nicholas was a gruff old chap who rode a bicycle to and from work and walked with a pronounced limp. He was universally rude to everybody, but constantly kind to me and to many of his black customers who came in for spares or repairs to their bicycles.

"You get up here on the counter and don't get in my way," he'd growl at me when I entered the shop.

And from my perch I'd watch in awe as he soldered a hole in a pressure stove, or tuned the spokes of a bicycle wheel or explained to me how a radio worked.

He always took the trouble to tell me what he was doing and why it had to be done just that way. Together we once built a crystal radio set, using just the bits and pieces lying on his counter, and tuned it in to listen to a broadcast from Grahamstown. It was sheer magic.

A farm labourer would wheel his rattling bicycle into the shop and hesitantly explain that it was wobbling and making a bad noise from the front wheel.

"That's because you don't look after your things," Mr Nicholas would snarl. "You have one of the most wonderful pieces of engineering ever invented and you treat it like rubbish. Leave it there and get out of my shop."

Hours later the owner would return hesitantly to claim his cycle. The wheel spokes would have been tightened and tuned, the fork bearings replaced and greased, the pedals straightened and everything properly aligned.

"How much do I owe the oubaas?" would come the anxious question.

"Oh, take the damn thing and buzz off. You can't afford to pay." And he would return to the task at hand without a further glance at his customer.

Like so many of the characters of a small Karoo town, David Nicholas had a story to tell. Sent off to boarding school in Grahamstown at the age of eight, he excelled at sport and study, although he admitted to me he had arrived with none of the refinements required of a city boy.

"The first thing I learned when I went to school," he once told me, "was that I was not allowed to throw stones at women. It was an extraordinary idea. I was beaten soundly in order to impress the lesson on me."

He must have polished up his social skills quite rapidly, because in 1908 he won a Rhodes scholarship and went to Oxford where he gained a degree in physics, chemistry and mathematics. He also won an Oxford Blue for rowing.

Rhodes scholars are selected for their all-round capabilities, leadership qualities, sporting achievements and, of course, academic excellence, so he must have been an exceptional young man.

With an Oxford degree and a Rhodes scholarship he could probably have walked into the pick of jobs in any international corporation. Instead he returned to Middelburg and took over the running of his late father's bicycle shop.

When the town switched from paraffin-operated streetlights to electricity, David Nicholas was the man who designed and installed the system.

Some of the streetlights he installed are probably in use to this day.

Nicholas never married, but lived with two spinster sisters, the Miss Halls. This, in a small country town, was the subject of endless speculation, but none of it spoken aloud. He was what was known then as a "fresh-air fiend" and liked to keep his bedroom window open all year round, even when the winter frost lay white on the morning grass. His bed was set on wheels and he had erected a fly screen cage around his window. At night he rolled the bed into position and slept with this head outside, in the cage.

Maybe it was this arrangement that kept him free from real gossip.

Even with the widest stretch of imagination, nobody could imagine him misbehaving sexually with his head outside the house in a fly screen cage.

COFFINS AND CRAZY CHARACTERS

I have often thought one of the cruellest things anybody could do to an author is to select one of his or her works as a school set-work book. In my matric year I was given Olive Schreiner's *Story of an African Farm* as a set book. I've hated it ever since. And her. I found the book dark and glum and the characters stodgy and unkind – not at all like the Karoo people I had come to know and love.

And, the more I have read about the author subsequently, the more convinced I have become that she was a self-centred lunatic. Who in their right mind would spend their lives lugging two coffins about with them wherever they went?

Olive Schreiner travelled everywhere with the corpses of her baby daughter and her dog, which had been run over by a carriage.

She bought a small plot of land right on the top of Buffelskop, near Cradock, one of the most inaccessible mountains in the whole Karoo, and decreed that she be buried there, along with her unnamed baby daughter and dead dog, Nita.

It took a team of twelve bearers two days to lug the coffins up the steep mountain after Olive's death in 1920. They slept next to the coffins that night, and ten of the bearers fled in terror during the night when baboons' barking echoed across the mountainside – as if it wasn't scary enough to be sleeping with three full coffins! They had to be rounded up (cowering in a farm shed) and persuaded to complete the journey the following day. The summit was composed of solid rock, so no grave could be dug there. A stonemason had been hired to erect a mausoleum instead and that wasn't much fun either, as it was mid-winter and the mortar froze between the laying of each stone. (Not to mention having to carry heavy bags of cement and buckets of icy water all the way up the mountain.)

The mason designed the tomb with a removable keystone, so Olive's estranged husband, Cron, could be buried in it later.

When his time came everybody had forgotten about the keystone and they smashed the well-built structure with sledge-hammers to get Cron's coffin inside. The original designer almost died of apoplexy when he heard of the sacrilege.

I can hardly imagine anybody causing more trouble and embarrassment than this crazy woman. And yet I was supposed to read her gloomy ramblings in order to pass my matric. I still bristle with indignation at the thought.

But I suppose the Karoo has produced more than its share of unconventional folk. Maybe it's the great silences echoing in their heads that make them strange.

Just visit the little village of Nieu-Bethesda near Graaff-Reinet and take a look at those weird conrete sculptures, some with religious themes, some from the poems of Omar Khayam, in the grounds of the Owl House, which is now a tourist attraction. Helen Martins dreamed up a menagerie of strange creatures and employed a wandering sheep-shearer, Koos Malgas, to turn them into reality, using a mixture of concrete and broken glass. The result is an unruly tangle of birds, camels, mythical creatures and staring glass-eyed faces.

Can anybody believe this was the work of a sane person?

Ironically, the eccentric Miss Martins was shunned by the village people during her life – or maybe she shunned them, who knows. But now her work is the town's main – and only – attraction and draws hundreds of curious visitors to the little hamlet each year.

She ended her life by swallowing caustic soda, which doesn't seem like the act of a completely sane person to me. It must have been an agonising death.

On a less gloomy note, when you drive from Cradock to Middelburg you may be interested in several tall chimneys that rise from the Karoo plains for no apparent reason. These were erected by a local farmer, Mr Charlie Hall, in an attempt to bring the rain. He believed that by sending up columns of specially formulated chemical smoke he would seed the passing clouds and make it rain.

Each time a promising cloud appeared in the sky, Mr Hall would rush out and light the prepared fires. Unfortunately the rain always fell somewhere else and the rainmaker tried in vain to get the recipients of the downpour to pay him for his efforts. Rainmaking chemicals don't come cheaply. Strangely the farmers who did get rain were not convinced that it was the same rain Mr Hall had created. One shower looks very much like another to a Karoo farmer.

Eventually the rainmaking project had to be abandoned for lack of funds.

Several delightfully eccentric characters arrived in the Karoo shortly after the British ended their rule in India. British army officers and senior officials who had served their Queen faithfully in India were offered the opportunity of being settled anywhere within the British Empire.

One such retired officer, a Colonel Murray, bought a small sheep farm near Middelburg and set up his home there, knowing nothing at all about farming.

Somebody once asked him why, of all the places in the Empire he could have chosen, he had decided to come to a sheep farm in the Karoo.

His reply was, "Well, y'see, I'm so beastly fond of kidneys."

Being a military man, he erected a smart red-and-white striped sentry box at the entrance to his farm, next to the main road. Whenever he had a letter he wanted posted, he would take it and march smartly down the road to his sentry box to stand stiffly to attention and await the first car to come by. At the approach of a car he would take two paces forward into the road, execute a right turn and a crisp salute. When the astonished motorist had skidded to a halt, and the dust settled, the good colonel would step up, hand over the letter, salute crisply and do an about-turn before marching stiffly back to his house.

I believe that most of the letters arrived safely at their destinations, because Karoo people are considerate and would not dream of allowing a letter to go unposted.

They know what it's like to have family living far away.

DANCING THE NIGHT AWAY

My teen years in the Karoo were the happiest of my life, and probably unbelievably innocent by today's standards.

The 1950s were the days of Elvis and Pat Boone on the radio, Lonnie Donegan and his Skiffle Group, the weekly Lourenço Marcques Radio *Hits of the Week*, and the arrival of the radiogram, forerunner to today's hi-fi sound system.

By now most of the farms had installed electric generators, which produced 32 volts of electricity that was stored in rows of glass batteries to provide instant light – a great advance from the paraffin lamps with which we grew up.

But far more important than light to us teenagers was the music. By fitting a large transformer, known as an "inverter", we could convert the 32-volt DC current to 220 volts AC – enough to power a Philips "Bi-ampli" radiogram, which combined a radio and record player. These were ornate affairs in imbuia wood, with linen-fold doors and ball-and-claw feet. The inverter produced a loud humming noise, so was usually installed outside on the stoep, where its noise didn't detract from the music. In a modernised version of the *opsit* courting tradition of yore, we teenagers would wait impatiently after supper until obliging parents yawned ostentatiously and betook themselves to bed, leaving the lounge free to the youngsters. Lights were turned down low and the radiogram was switched on for us young couples to listen to, holding hands in the gloom and sometimes daringly stealing a kiss to the strains of Elvis singing "Love me Tender".

My mother later told us she used to listen to the hum of the inverter and knew exactly when we finally switched off and tiptoed up to bed. She always referred to it as the "informer."

All of us farm lads learned to drive the truck as soon as our legs were long enough to allow us to reach the brake and clutch pedals. Karoo country roads carried very little traffic, so fathers were usually generous in allowing us to drive off to neighbouring farms to visit our friends. And, of course, their sisters.

Summer school holidays were a time of teenage dances and weekends of swimming and tennis parties, and we thought nothing of travelling a hundred kilometres or more to a dance on a farm in the Middelburg, Steynsburg or Hanover district.

Life was safer then and parents felt confident that we would return unharmed in the early hours of the morning. They seldom sat up waiting for us.

One such party was to be held in the Steynsburg Town Hall, some one hundred kilometres away, and my friend André Pienaar had arranged to borrow his dad's rather spectacular Studebaker Hawk for the trip.

(Families had their favourite makes of car – all American, because they were large and heavy and stood up well to the rough Karoo roads. We always had Chevrolets. The Pienaars were Studebaker people. The racehorse breeder went in for fancier makes, like Oldsmobiles or Cadillacs.)

I was going with him and taking my first serious girlfriend, Mary-Anne, a Port Elizabeth girl who was spending her summer holiday on a neighbouring farm.

Without wishing to be too boastful, she and I were known for our energetic rock'n'roll performances on the dance floor and the ooms and tannies used to line the hall and applaud when we were on top form.

Preparation for a dance was a serious business. Nice girls wore stockings in those days, hidden under layer upon layer of stiff petticoats that always posed a problem in the confines of a car. Usually they were carried in a pillowslip in the boot of the car until we'd reached the party destination, and then hurriedly rustled round to the ladies' room to be slipped on.

Stockings were uncomfortably hot in the Karoo summers, so Mary-Anne hit on a cool solution to the problem. She used to get me to paint a heel and seam on the back of each leg with watercolour.

We were both keen artists.

Voilà! Perfect stockings.

And of course the excitement of painting those seams was almost too much to bear. Just how high up was I permitted to paint as she stood on a table and held her skirt out of the way?

But I digress.

The three of us set off for Steynsburg and enjoyed as fine an evening of dancing and swaggering as ever. Nobody knew about drugs in those days, although some of the more daring lads would sneak off for a surreptitious cigarette round the side of the hall, and some of the older boys had probably swiped a couple of beers from their parents' drinks cupboards.

That was naughtiness enough.

After midnight the three of us boarded the Studebaker and André started on the homeward journey. It seemed to be taking a very long time and the road, in the dark, appeared unfamiliar, but we assured each other we knew where we were. André spotted what he thought was a familiar landmark and announced that he knew exactly where we now were.

"In fact, there's a short cut just a bit further, that takes us right through to Vlakfontein. We'll take that."

Some moments later the Studebaker crested a small hill and we plunged suddenly and unexpectedly into a swiftly flowing river.

This hadn't been in André's original calculation.

The car's long nose submerged and there was a ripping noise as the fan, bent by the force of water, tore a large hole in the radiator. Mary-Anne, always resourceful, suggested we simply stay in the car until dawn and then assess the situation when it was light. The thought of a whole night on the back seat with her quickly added my vote to her suggestion and we settled down to sleep while the muddy water oozed under the doors and filled the floor of the car.

At first light we paddled out to inspect the damage. A small cake of soap (Mary-Anne's) and a strip torn from a petticoat (obviously Mary-Anne's) made a temporary plug for the holed radiator and we were soon on our way.

Nobody seemed concerned when we arrived home well after breakfast. Each parent simply assumed that we had stayed over at one of the other farms.

Such was the trust and innocence of the time.

Volkswagens and Tickey Fords

For any young man starting a farming career in the Karoo, some sort of vehicle is essential. The farms are far apart and far from town and, unless a young fellow has wheels, he's likely to lose contact with the rest of the world.

Nobody wants to be a hermit.

In the 1950s and '60s my father took in two nephews as "learner farmers". In a system rather like the apprentice system used in other trades, the learner farmers would help around the farm wherever needed and eventually be sent to an agricultural college. In our case it was always Grootfontein Agricultural College in Middelburg, as it offered a specialised two-year course in sheep and wool farming.

The first of our learners was my cousin Reed Howes, whose family had lived next door on Kenilworth until his mother, Aunt Elma, sold it to Dad and moved to Cape Town with her two teenage children, Reed and June.

But Reed's heart was always set on farming, so it was natural that he come to Grapevale as a learner farmer as soon as he finished his schooling at Bishops.

My father was a natural teacher, always ready to explain anything that needed explanation, and always infinitely patient. I believe this is partly why Reed's farming career was so successful.

But of course he needed transport, and his first vehicle was a magnificent black AJS 500cc single cylinder motorcycle.

Reed was tall, good-looking and popular, great company and an excellent tennis and cricket player. I was about thirteen years old at the time and it was no wonder I regarded him with complete awe. It was probably from that time that I developed my lifelong affection for motorcycles, and particularly older models.

Reed would travel the sixty or so kilometres from the farm to Colesberg on his AJS every Saturday evening to meet the young bucks of the district at the Central Hotel for a few beers before going to the local "bioscope" to watch the week's film.

On one memorable occasion he invited me to accompany him and I was in seventh heaven. However, it couldn't have been too much fun for him to have a hero-worshipping little teenager on his hands when he wanted to enjoy a beer and some men's talk with his pals, so he slipped me the bike key and said, "Here, Boetie, take the AJ for a spin."

I almost fainted with joy. I'd never ridden before, but had seen how it was done.

We wore no helmets in those easy times and obviously I had no licence to ride the machine, but nobody in his right mind would pass up an opportunity like that. I straddled the heavy bike and managed to kick it into life, get it in gear and set off along the town's main road toward the church. Round the church I went and then approached the rather steep hill known as "Vaalbank". Here I some-how failed to get into the correct gear and stalled the motor.

It was a frightening moment. I needed all my small strength just to keep the bike upright on the steep road and, whenever I tried to kick-start it, it would begin rolling downhill backwards and threatening to fall over.

I eventually reached the bottom of the hill, by means of short backward wobbles, a few metres at a time, and stood there, trembling and exhausted, while I tried to catch my breath. After a great deal of huffing and

puffing and kicking I managed to restart the machine and turn it round for the home run to the pub. Reed looked up as I strolled in, trying to look nonchalant.

"You were out for quite a while," he said approvingly. "Have a good ride?"

"Fantastic!" I lied. "She goes like a bomb."

"Come on," he said, "I'll buy you a beer before we go to the flick."

Oh wow! A beer! Suddenly I was one of the manne. I had ridden the AJ, now I was offered a beer.

Paradise was regained.

Later, of course, romance stirred and it became necessary for a self-respecting young man to own a car. You can't take a girlfriend out with any dignity on a motorbike. Besides, the riding position limits romantic possibilities.

The only available small cars in the Karoo in those days were the Volkswagen Beetle and the Morris Minor. The Morris was frankly not up to surviving the corrugated Karoo roads, so almost every young farmer started his motoring career with a Volksie Beetle.

You could save quite a bit of money in those days by collecting your car straight from the factory in Uitenhage, instead of having it delivered to the dealer in town.

Reed – ever indulgent toward his pesky young cousin – invited me to accompany him on his train trip to Uitenhage to collect his very first Volksie.

It was blue and smelled wonderfully new, but was still coated with a thick layer of brown protective wax, which we had to have removed at one of the garages near the factory.

Then it was ready to go.

The first drive was to Collegiate Girls' School where Reed's girlfriend, Anne, was a boarder. Obviously this was a momentous occasion for her too – imagine, to be collected for an outing by a boyfriend who owned his own car!

As we parked in front of the school we could see several curtains twitching as Anne's classmates peered out surreptitiously to inspect the wonderful boyfriend. She was ushered into the car gallantly and Reed got in behind the wheel and started the engine. As it was a two-door I was already in the back seat.

The car revved and revved, hesitated, revved again, almost climbed on to the pavement, hesitated and revved again.

Reed couldn't find reverse gear.

Somewhat embarrassed, we all climbed out and pushed the car out of the parking space, got in again and drove off.

Somehow the gloss had gone from the moment. Maybe it was simply a case of pride coming before a fall.

A minor one, admittedly.

Reed and Anne later married happily and raised three charming daughters, so the Volksie incident was a mere hiccup along the corrugated road of life.

Long before the advent of the Beetle, the Model T Ford was the first car of almost every driver in the country. It was also the only car cheap enough for young farmers to afford. My father remembered that a Model T could be bought new in 1923 for less than one hundred and sixty pounds. Their low price earned them the nickname of "tickey Fords" (a tickey was a three-penny coin).

Spares were cheap too and the Graaff-Reinet Ford dealer used to claim that he could assemble a whole Model T from spare parts for almost the same price as a new car. Just try that exercise today!

One of Dad's early memories was a visit to the Ford factory in Port Elizabeth during his schooldays at Grey College. He wrote his impressions of that visit for me many years later.

"The factory was turning out a stream of twenty-four cars a day – one every half hour," he wrote. "It seemed a staggering number and we reckoned every adult in Port Elizabeth would be owning one soon."

His most vivid impression was of the painting shop.

"All standard Model Ts came in one colour – black. In the duco-painting section the speed of painting was very fast. The car body was slung from overhead rails. A supply tank of black paint hung about two metres above the body. A rubber hose was connected to the tank and to this was fixed a length of steel pipe perforated with small holes, like an elongated showerhead.

"The painter simply guided this paint shower over the car body, coating it generously, and the surplus paint poured down and dripped into a concrete trough below the body. "This surplus was pumped back into the overhead tank by an operator seated on a fixed bicycle and pedalling away like mad. A belt attached to the raised wheel drove the paint pump, so the paint was never wasted.

"The painted bodies were drip-dried and, behold, a shiny new black Model T was ready to be mounted on its chassis."

An interesting feature of those early Fords was that they had no batteries for lighting. The engine-driven generator sent electricity directly to the headlamps when needed.

"This meant, the faster the speed at which you travelled, the brighter your lights were. Roads in the country were pretty bad so, when the driver slowed down to negotiate a particularly tricky part, the car's lights dimmed to almost nothing, unless the engine was revved up from time to time to illuminate the way ahead."

And we complain about our vehicles today.

But there was a good side to those early Ford days.

"Mechanics were few and far apart and most repairs were carried out by the owners," Dad writes. "It was quite amazing how many repairs could be done with just a pair of pliers and some wire."

And today's cars need a special computer to diagnose even a minor fault, after which you can't repair it anyway. You have to replace the faulty part and are then told you can't buy just the broken bit as it comes as "part of a complete unit", so it costs an arm and both legs.

That's progress, I suppose. We win some, we lose some.

MOTORBIKES, MINISTERS AND MUSCADEL

I was rather surprised when, in 1978, I found myself in the post of official wine writer for the *Cape Argus* newspaper in Cape Town. Fate plays some strange tricks on us.

Until then I had always considered myself to be almost exclusively a beer drinker. Wine has not played a major role in our family's history, although we did try to make our own wine one year when the Crystal grapes on the farm vines had produced a particularly good crop. We harvested the ripe golden berries and pressed them by hand in the large tin bathtub normally used for the family laundry.

After straining out the largest of the lumps, we added some yeast from the pantry and poured the result into several tall glass jars that had once housed the batteries for the farm's 32-volt lighting system.

Here the juice fermented for a while, after which Dad sealed each jar firmly, using a square of plywood stuck in place with Genkem contact adhesive. When we reckoned it was ready for bottling, it was decanted into a variety of screw-cap bottles and laid down to mature.

Some time later the first of the bottles was opened and tasted.

The result was too dreadful for words. The only aroma that had come through was that of the contact adhesive. The wine became known as our "Genkem Wine" and was carefully avoided.

My father came from a family of Baptist and Quaker teetotallers, whereas my mother's people enjoyed an occasional glass of the good stuff. Dad probably took his first glass of wine more to please his future in-laws than himself.

Once they were married, however, my parents enjoyed the occasional drink, and it became their happy habit to settle down to a glass or two at the end of every long working day. Dad developed his own favourite drink – whisky and lemonade – and Mom liked a glass of gin and tonic. Once a year this pleasant ritual was disrupted for a week or two when Uncle Billy came to stay.

Uncle Billy Doke was a stern man with a bristling little Hitler-type moustache, who had risen to the exalted position of General Secretary of the Baptist Union of South Africa. He was a disapprover by nature.

I remember his early visits to the farm very vividly.

At sunset my parents would announce that they were going upstairs to bath and dress for dinner, and would then sneak up, pour themselves a glass each and sit uncomfortably on the edge of the bath, sipping and chatting while Uncle Billy waited downstairs for his supper and prayers.

Eventually my mother had had enough.

"This is *my* home, dammit," she said, "and I'm jolly well going to enjoy my usual drink in the evening."

This was duly announced in gentler terms to Uncle Billy the next evening. His little moustache quivered in disapproval for a moment. Then he decided he would go for a little walk while the naughtiness was committed. After a while he became more accustomed to the idea and, seeing that no lightning struck the house of wickedness each evening, decided to join the enemy and have a glass of orange squash with them.

I believe he actually came to enjoy the evening ritual.

His evening family prayer sessions did seem to go on rather longer than usual after that, though.

We Biggses have rather a sweet tooth and most of the family enjoy a glass of fortified hanepoot jerepigo or muscadel. My Dad always said he liked any wine, as long as he could put in a splash of hanepoot to sweeten it.

One hot summer afternoon I set off on the eight hundred-kilometre journey from Cape Town on my motorcycle, to spend a weekend on the farm.

There's not much luggage space on a motorbike but I stopped at Du Toitskloof Cellar near Worcester and managed to squeeze six bottles of their charming hanepoot jerepigo into my pannier bags.

The kilometres slipped by and the afternoon sun beat down with the usual Karoo sting. I decided to spend the night in Beaufort West and found a quiet room that opened onto a courtyard with a large peppercorn tree in the middle.

After the long hot ride I seriously needed some refreshment and took out a bottle of the rather warm hanepoot and set it in the basin to cool.

Later, as I sat in the shade of the peppercorn tree sipping the sweet wine, a carload of travellers from Johannesburg arrived, all looking hot and tired. They eyed my bottle enviously and of course I invited them to pull up a glass and join me. This they did without hesitation.

Another traveller joined us and I opened a second bottle.

The evening ended up in high good spirits. Time and hanepoot slipped by and we parted around midnight, the very best of friends.

The next day my brother seemed slightly underwhelmed by my gift.

"I know you were on the bike," he complained, "but, even so, I do think you could have fitted more than just the *one* bottle in your carrier bag."

I now make a point of travelling by car.

THE GREAT FLOOD

As you drive through Laingsburg on a hot summer day, it's hard to believe that the dusty little town was once almost completely destroyed by the worst flood ever experienced in the Karoo. More than a hundred people died in the flood and about half the houses in the town were washed away or damaged beyond repair.

Today a sign in Laingsburg's main street, far from the riverbed, proclaims "High Water Mark". It's difficult to imagine water in those hot, dusty streets at all, let alone so far from the river.

I often wondered how so many people could have drowned in the 1981 flood. Surely, I thought to myself, anybody seeing the water rising over the riverbanks would have the common sense to move to higher ground?

I must have been missing something in the story. So I took a trip to the town and spoke to some of the flood survivors. Their stories are harrowing and their memories painfully real even all these years after the event.

Like so many natural events in the Karoo, the 1981 flood was swift and violent.

The average rainfall in the district is a meagre one hundred and seventy-five millimetres a year. But on that occasion four hundred and twenty-five millimetres of rail fell in two days, creating a virtual wall of speeding water that carried everything in front of it – uprooted trees, drowned cattle and pieces of farm buildings tumbled along in the torrent.

Three riverbeds join together at Laingsburg – the Wilgehout, Baviaans and Buffalo rivers. When the head of the flood reached the town the combined might of the three rivers was far too powerful to be contained in the riverbed, and part of it spread to streets that ran parallel to the riverbed.

People found their homes cut off from the rest of the town and tried to make their way to higher ground, but were swept off their feet and hurled into the flood while others watched helplessly.

As the waters rose, trapped families climbed onto their roofs. But the old walls could not withstand the pressure of water and slowly the houses sagged and collapsed, depositing their human refugees into the water to be swept away.

Nearly two hundred houses were destroyed.

One villager told me he had watched as a house came loose from its foundations and slowly began to swivel until its front door was no longer facing the street. Then it sagged and fell and was swallowed up, together with the people on it.

The last building to go was the home for the aged and there are many local stories of heroism as people battled in vain to save the lives of the elderly residents.

One of them was the Dutch Reformed pastor, Rev Malan Jacobs, who was drowned while trying to rescue the elderly. Some of the aged clung to trees, trying to escape the force of the river, but they were soon ripped off and sent hurtling into the flood. There are also stories of miraculous escapes and ten people were rescued, battered but alive, in the Floriskraal Dam a whole twenty-one kilometres from the town.

For those less lucky, bodies were simply swept away. Some were never recovered and some were found as far away as Mossel Bay.

In Cape Town the newspaper *Die Burger* started a fund for the flood victims and collected three million rands. The government spent another seven million rebuilding houses and repairing damage to the town.

Apart from the signposts, there are few traces of the disaster left today and the town goes about its peaceful way like any other sleepy Karoo dorp.

Along the riverbank, where the flood once spread its muddy swath of chaos and death, a green golf course has been built. Players say they can still see indentations in the grassed fairways, which mark the places where houses fell.

FINGERS TO THE SKY

The route from Beaufort West to Aberdeen is one of the most desolate stretches of road I know. For more than one hundred and twenty kilometres the narrow ribbon of asphalt lies arrow-straight across a landscape that's flat, grey and featureless. Here and there small clumps of white-thorned acacia trees provide the flocks of sheep and angora goats with a little shade from the merciless Karoo sun but, for the rest, nothing – stunted grey scrub, gravel and stones. Even the occasional farmstead, way off in the distance, appears empty and abandoned.

For all its appearance of being deserted, this country – called the Camdeboo – supports large and prosperous sheep farms. Such is the magic of the Karoo.

Even here of course the impression of emptiness is an illusion. Stop at the roadside and you're likely to see scurrying families of bright-eyed vervet monkeys scampering for the safety of the nearest mimosa tree.

What do they live on in this endless wilderness?

Inquisitive meerkats pop up from their burrows and sit bolt upright to survey the intruder before flashing back down to safety.

After what seems like an eternity, the tall white spire of the Aberdeen Dutch Reformed Church appears in the distance. Like most little Karoo towns, the village of Aberdeen clusters round its church.

In this case even the name of the town has church connections. It is derived from Aberdeen in Scotland, birthplace of the Reverend Andrew Murray, who probably did more than any other pioneer churchman to spread the Christian religion across southern Africa. It's no wonder the town's steeple can be seen from so far off.

Residents of Aberdeen are quick to tell you that theirs is the tallest steeple of any church in South Africa. What they probably won't tell you is that the tip of their steeple is actually almost half a metre out of plumb.

These things are accepted where country labour is involved.

From Aberdeen to Graaff-Reinet the road becomes more interesting, winding through some spectacular mountain scenery, offering stunning views of the great plains of the Camdeboo.

Graaff-Reinet is one of the most historically aware towns in the country. Whole streets have been restored and the well-known National Monuments plaque can be seen on many of the buildings. One such street is now called the Drostdyhof, formerly Stretch's Court. It consists of thirteen small cottages originally given to freed slaves by their former owner, Captain Charles Stretch. They are now part of the Drostdy Hotel complex.

My first memory of Graaff-Reinet goes back to 1947, when the British royal family were on their state visit to South Africa to thank the people of this country for their contribution to the Allied efforts in World War II.

Many local farmers and businessmen from Graaff-Reinet had served – and some had died – in the Middellandse Regiment, proudly referred to as the DMR. The regiment was captured at the fall of Tobruk.

Royalism was at a high peak in those triumphant post-war times and Graaff-Reinet was the closest town to our home that the royal entourage would visit.

Very early in the morning the entire farm population – our family and farm staff – set off on every available vehicle for the one hundred and twenty-kilometre journey to see the King and Queen. We lined up on the steps in front of Graaff-Reinet's ornate church and waited in the hot sun.

Eventually the cavalcade arrived and there were their majesties, King George VI and Queen Elizabeth, sitting in an open black car and waving graciously to the crowds. It was all over in a few moments, of course, and we were soon on our way back home. To the farm staff it had been a great disappointment.

"I don't think that was the king at all," said Menziwe Ntame, our tractor driver, on the way home. "A king wears long robes and a gold hat with jewels on it. I have seen this in many pictures. That man was dressed the same as I dress when I go to church. It was definitely not the king. Maybe the king sent his assistant. Maybe he did not think the people of Graaff-Reinet were important enough."

It was a debate that lasted many weeks, as Karoo debates are wont to do.

The Dutch Reformed Church in front of which we stood is an impressive and ornate building, modelled on the design of Salisbury Cathedral in England.

One minor change is that the church in Graaff-Reinet is one of very few churches in the country to have a chimney.

It's not unusual for Karoo churches to have their origins in Europe.

The Dutch Reformed Church in Cradock for example, is said to be a smaller version of the church of St Martin-in-the-Fields in London.

After all, why go to all the bother of designing a church from scratch when others have done such an admirable job?

ANOTHER ROYAL KAROO VISIT

In spite of our republican leanings, South Africans it seems have always nurtured a deep respect for royalty. When Prince Edward, who later gave up his throne for his forbidden love of an American divorcée, visited South African in 1925, he was greeted everywhere with respect and honour by English- and Afrikaans-speaking people alike.

In Burgersdorp, for example, a rather frosty reception was expected, because the folk of that town were almost all Afrikaners and had fought against the British in the South African War.

To their surprise a great arch of greenery had been erected in the town square and solemn speeches of welcome were delivered by the mayor after lengthy prayers of thanks for the royal visit by the dominee.

They all expressed the thought that, under different circumstance, English and Afrikaans South Africans could have lived together in peace and harmony.

A day-by-day account of the official tour of South Africa was published shortly afterwards by G Ward Price, who accompanied the prince (*Through South Africa with The Prince,* The Gill Publishing Co Ltd, London, 1926). In it, he describes a weekend spent in the Colesberg district on the farm of Sir Abe Bailey, Grootfontein, which is some fifteen kilometres from my family's farm, Grapevale.

Grootfontein was the headquarters of the Bailey Agricultural Estates, and a special suite of rooms had been built specially to accommodate the prince and his entourage.

"Sir Abe Bailey," Price writes, "is one of the wealthiest men in South Africa, with widespread mining, stock-breeding and newspaper interests.

"His Colesberg property is an instance of how capital can tame the wilderness. Water is brought to fertilise the soil from deep boreholes, by means of those ugly galvanised iron windmills which are an almost invariable feature of any South African landscape, with their rattling flanges raised on sixty-foot tripod legs high above the trees."

In the front of the little book is a photograph of the prince mounted on a fine black horse, with the caption: "H.R.H. The Prince at Grootfontein".

There's a little story behind that picture. The Pienaar family, who have owned the adjoining farm, Weltevrede, for generations, have a precious souvenir of that royal visit – a shiny gold cigarette case presented to Grandfather Piet Pienaar in gratitude for the loan of his fine horse. The horse, called Critic, was well known as one of the finest riding horses in the district and certainly fit for a prince.

My father once wrote to me about that memorable royal visit:

"The prince seemed more interested in riding this splendid horse than he did in the springbok hunt that had been arranged for his benefit. During the lunch break when the hunters had gathered for refreshments, a large springbok ram came running past at full speed, about to pass the picnic party about three hundred metres away. Piet Pienaar was a fine marksman and somebody handed him a rifle and said, half jokingly: 'Come on Piet. Have a shot at it.'

"Piet took aim, fired and the buck dropped dead in its tracks. He handed back the rifle and said, 'I got him through the neck.'

"Somebody was sent to collect the dead animal and it was indeed shot through the neck as Mr Pienaar had said. The prince was amazed at such accuracy, and also at the fact that Mr Pienaar had been able to see, at 300 yards, exactly where the bullet had hit the buck.

"Later Oom Piet confessed that he hadn't actually aimed at the neck and couldn't really see where the shot had struck, but knew by the way the springbok fell that it must have been a neck shot.

"Some time later a package arrived from Buckingham Palace addressed to Mr PA Pienaar and inside was a photograph of the prince astride Critic and a gold cigarette case bearing the royal coat of arms."

His daughter-in-law, Aunt Rita Pienaar, of Scottish descent and a staunch royalist, often used to show the cigarette case to visitors and tell how it came into the family. Obviously an item of rare value, it was kept in a glass display cabinet with other family treasures.

Some years ago an "antiques roadshow" came to the district, and local residents were invited to bring their treasures for evaluation.

Not many families can boast a gift presented by grateful royalty, so the cigarette case was duly submitted for scrutiny.

To Aunt Rita's disappointment the evaluator said it was one of many similar cases that had been produced in Birmingham and was not worth a great deal of money. The precious heirloom had lost a bit of its gloss, but certainly none of its sentimental value.

Sometimes it's best not to have our illusions tarnished by mere facts.

And, indeed, later events certainly did tarnish the prince's royal reputation.

Lynette Barling of Fish Hoek told me her own story of that royal visit.

She was a young girl living with her parents in Kimberley at the time. Her father, a former officer in the Black Watch regiment, was one of the dignitaries invited to attend the official welcoming function for the prince and his entourage at the Kimberley Club.

They duly set off in the family's grand old Graham-Page car, dressed in all their finery and medals.

Not long afterwards they returned home, rather earlier than expected and slightly dishevelled, and the excited young Lynette rushed out to find out what had happened. What had the prince said? What had he been wearing? What did they serve for dinner?

Her parents spoke a few terse words to each other in French, as they did when they did not want the children to understand. Then her mother took her aside and told her never, ever to mention to anybody, on pain of death, what had happened.

Apparently the prince and his cronies had arrived at the club rather the worse for wear, found the garden hose curled up on the lawn and turned it on. They then proceeded to spray the water through the open windows, drenching the assembled dignitaries inside and howling with drunken laughter.

After they had been discreetly whisked away to their hotel, the mayor made a brief speech saying that the prince was obviously very tired and emotional after his strenuous schedule, and it was hoped that nobody present would mention this regrettable incident.

Significantly, no mention is made of that official function in Price's book.

The remarkable thing was that nobody ever did mention the incident in public (until Lynette spilled the beans to me more than sixty years later).

One can't help wondering what today's tabloid press would have made of it: "Drunken Royals in Messy Club Fracas. Photos on pages 3, 4 and 5."

Maybe the British royal family is no worse today than its forebears, in spite of divorces and all-too public scandals. The difference is that in 1925 the public was prepared to believe the fairy tales of the handsome princes and beautiful princesses who were above ordinary folk and would certainly live happily ever after.

And maybe we're the poorer for our loss of illusions.

History on the Roadside

The bumpy gravel road from Noupoort to Oorlogspoort takes you up and up into the folds of the Holbrook Heights, where it snows almost every winter. And sometimes little families of nomadic "*karretjiemense*" are caught in the blizzard and children have been known to freeze to death.

These wandering families are a feature of the Karoo. With their meagre belongings piled on a dilapidated cart drawn by a scrawny donkey or two, they leave their wobbly tracks along the country roads from farm to farm, finding odd jobs here and there, but never settling for long in one place.

Some of the small yellow-skinned men are experts at fixing fences; others can shear a sheep with great skill. The typical *karretjietrek* includes at least one thin, curly-tailed dog loping along behind the cart and a chicken or two swinging in a wire cage slung underneath alongside the dented teakettle.

When night falls the trek halts and the leader arranges a few sheets of battered corrugated iron into a shelter with the cart acting as its roof. The campfire is lit and that's home for the next night or two – or until an anxious farmer orders them to move along. They are not above catching and skinning the occasional sheep to roast for their supper when the dog has failed to rustle up a hare.

It's a tough way of life, but the "people of the road" prefer it to any kind of settled lifestyle.

From time to time my family has offered permanent employment and a proper house to one of these wandering families, and they have accepted and settled down for a short while. But invariably the day dawns when the house is found empty and the tracks of the cart can be seen vanishing into the distance.

Ask them why they left and they shrug and say: *"Die pad het geroep, seur."* (The road called us, sir.)

Not many cars use the winding road through the Holbrook mountains but, for those who do, there's a story that runs alongside it.

Before the days of chain stores, where every town and village now contains the same range of shops – branches of big-city stores or franchised stores – shop-keepers did their own buying and every shop offered a unique selection of goods.

Noupoort's biggest general dealer's store belonged to a wealthy resident who also owned the large Holbrook farm. In about 1920 he set off on his annual buying trip overseas and chanced upon what he considered the bargain of a lifetime.

Britain's War Department had produced thousands of miles of barbed wire for use in the muddy trenches of France during World War I.

Now the battles were over and the wire lay in jagged mountains in army surplus depots, no longer needed. Our storekeeper managed to buy tons of it for a very small price and had it shipped back for sale to the local farmers.

There was a snag, however, as there so often is with bargains. The barbed wire was not galvanised. It had not been made to last. Trenches moved with the sway of war, and barbed wire entanglements were laid down, and then abandoned when the soldiers advanced or retreated.

Noupoort's farmers took one look and shook their heads. Who would use ungalvanised wire? There were no takers.

Eventually, to make the best of a bad job, the shopkeeper carted the ungalvanised wire out to Holbrook and used it in his own boundary fences, where they survive to this day.

Take a look at those fences if you're ever on that road.

The barbs are closer together than the normal barbs used for stock fences. They were designed to keep out humans, not sheep. And there are four or five strands of barbed wire in the fence instead of the usual one strand at the top.

There was a great deal of wire to be used.

But the most interesting thing of all is that it didn't rust.

The air of the Karoo is so dry that rust is not a problem. A thin, hard film of polished oxide forms and seals the steel against further corrosion.

Almost a century later, that barbed wire is as good as it was when it menaced the German soldiers on the muddy battlefields of Flanders, Ypres and the Somme.

TREK BOKKEN AND TAK BOKKEN

In his wonderful book *Wild Sports of Southern Africa*, published in 1852, Captain William Cornwallis Harris describes the vast herds of springbok that grazed on the open veld near Graaff-Reinet.

"Here the face of the country was literally white with spring-bucks, myriads of which covered the plains, affording us a welcome supply of food. When hunted, these elegant creatures take extraordinary bounds, rising with curved backs high into the air, as if about to take flight: and they invariably clear a road or beaten track in this manner, as if their natural disposition to regard man as an enemy, induced them to mistrust even the ground upon which he had trod."

He describes the enormous migrations of springbok across the wide Karoo plains.

"The 'trek bokken', as the occasional immigration of these antelopes is called by the colonists, may be reckoned amongst the most extraordinary examples of the fecundity of animal life. To offer any estimate of their numbers would be impossible: pouring down like locusts from the endless plains of the interior, whence they have been driven by protracted drought, lions have been seen stalking in the middle of their compressed phalanx, and flocks of sheep have not infrequently been carried away by the torrent."

Another writer of that time described how an apparently endless river of game had taken three days, running at full speed, to pass the spot where he had camped.

Obviously all that changed as soon as the first fence was erected around a farm.

Today there are small herds of springbok on almost every Karoo farm and, because most modern farmers take great care not to over-graze their precious veld, it is seldom necessary for the springbok to seek food elsewhere.

We will not see migrations like those again.

But there have been interesting animal migrations of a different kind across the Karoo. One of my earliest memories of moving to Grahamstown to attend boarding school (apart from the heartbreak of homesickness) was the weird, mocking call of the hadeda ibis. Its raucous "ha-haaa" was unlike anything I had ever heard on the farm.

The distribution map of the hadeda in my 1958 *Roberts' Birds of South Africa* extends from KwaZulu-Natal only as far as Port Elizabeth. Today the hadedas have spread right across the country and are a common sight and sound on most of the farms in the Colesberg and Middelburg districts, and even as far as Cape Town, so they certainly do get around.

(In my old edition of *Roberts' Birds* the hadeda has the most impressive Latin name of *Hagedashia hagedash hagedash*.)

Kudus, too, were unknown on our farm in those childhood years.

We were invited to hunt them once a year on my Uncle Llewellyn's farm, Wellfound, in the Graaff-Reinet district and they seemed huge and alien creatures to me. I had never seen anything as imposing.

They were officially listed as vermin at one time because of the destruction they caused to farmlands.

Today there are quite large herds of kudu roaming the farms in our area.

For all its large size, a kudu can clear an ordinary metre-and-a-half fence without the slightest effort. One moment the animal is standing on one side of the fence and the next he has simply floated over and landed gracefully on the other side. For anybody trying to grow fields of lucerne, like our neighbour, Tommy van der Walt, kudus have become a serious problem. Nobody ever needed to build high kudu fences in our area of the Karoo in the past.

Then there are some really unusual animals that have migrated across the Karoo in recent times. One day not so long ago one of the neighbours reported that he had seen a reindeer in the headlights of his truck as he returned from Colesberg a few nights before. Of course he was mocked unmercifully.

"Oh, come on, man! What did you have to drink before you left town?"

"No, seriously, man. It was a reindeer. It had bloody great antlers on its head."

But that merely increased the mockery, so he dropped the subject and kept his conviction to himself.

Some time later another neighbour reported seeing a deer with antlers.

"Aha! So now who's been drinking?"

Today it is not unusual to see several of these graceful deer grazing on the roadside. They have been identified as fallow deer and were apparently imported to the Karoo by a farmer near Schoombee, which is a small railway siding between Middelburg and Steynsburg. He probably wanted them as decorative pets to have around his home. They obviously enjoyed the Karoo climate and grazing and have multiplied and travelled widely.

It takes more than a mere fence to keep an antelope or deer in one area.

In recent times several wealthy city people – or groups of businessmen – have established game farms in the Karoo, often on farms that have proved unsuitable for raising sheep or cattle successfully. Some are run on strictly commercial lines, where herds of game are kept for hunting, at a set fee per species. They are properly managed and numbers are kept to set limits. Others are established mainly for the pleasure of their owners and guests as a retreat where they can enjoy a break from city life watching the animals in their natural surroundings.

There can be few better ways of recharging one's mental batteries.

Tall game fences are erected all round the boundaries of these game farms, but Mother Nature abhors a fence and the occasional animal escapes from time to time.

Sometimes a heavy Karoo storm will wash away the riverbed under a fence, creating a suitable buck-sized gap. Sometimes a large antelope, like an eland or wildebeest, will simply worry a fence until the wires part.

At the time of writing, my brother had an uninvited population of red hartebeest, several eland and a few impala roaming the farm. He reported their arrival to the owner of the game farm, but was secretly rather pleased to have the newcomers around.

Repeated attempts at herding them back to their home farm, Brulberg, have proved unsuccessful, even with a helicopter being used for the roundup. The escapers simply scatter, disappearing into the many deep gullies and riverbeds until the chase is over, then appearing a few days later, nonchalantly munching the grass and looking completely at home.

It will be interesting to see how the wildlife population of the Karoo changes in the next decade or two. My guess is that there will be herds of buck all over the area, where they have not been seen in generations. I can't believe this is a bad thing. On the vast spaces of the Karoo there's plenty of room for all.

Some time ago a young visitor to the farm came tearing back from an outing in the veld, wide-eyed, breathless and excited.

"Uncle Roger," he panted, "I have just seen a reindeer in the vlei."

"Yes, I know," said my brother calmly. "We keep them there so Santa Claus can replace his tired ones when he passes this way on Christmas Eve."

Karoo people do appreciate a good story.

THERE WERE SHEPHERDS
KEEPING WATCH OVER
THEIR FLOCKS BY NIGHT

December arrived and the farmers and their families decided to stage a nativity play shortly before Christmas. The younger children, of course, had all taken part in nativity plays at their schools, but this was to be an adult play. A serious, well produced show.

This was to be the play to end all Christmas plays, and why not? We had everything the story demanded – real shepherds, real sheep, horses and cows. One of the neighbours even produced a small donkey.

The production committee agreed the venue was to be our front garden, which had a convenient rustic summerhouse to use as a stable, several large pine trees to act as scenery and a nice comfortable slope so the audience would all be able to see. Everybody was involved, black and white. Rehearsals tended toward the hilarious, but we got the general idea. The choir practised together but failed to reach anything resembling harmony. Black singers and white singers use completely different voice techniques, and they combined to produce a fearful wailing noise. It was mutually agreed that there would be two parts of the choir and the carols would be sung alternately by the black singers and white singers.

Farm workshops hummed with activity as the cast built the crib, and made props – a lantern for the inn-keeper, crowns for the three kings, shepherds' crooks and special effects lighting arrangements.

Invitations were sent to surrounding areas, offering a grand spectacle followed by drinks and a braai. Replies poured in.

The grand opening night was upon us all too soon and the lighting was tested one last time before dusk.

Curtain up.

Perched in the fork of a convenient peach tree, Dad was ready with his spotlight – the headlight from an old Ford lorry.

Mary and Joseph (Lyn and Kenneth Dell) came wearily across the lawn. Mary, with a fat pillow tucked in her robe, balanced precariously on the reluctant donkey and Joseph was doing his best to steady the beast. After being spurned by the innkeeper and consigned to the stable, Mary surreptitiously exchanged the pillow for a very pink plastic doll and the choir of angels standing on tables behind the summerhouse rose up and sang a bilingual Hallelujah.

Up on the balcony a concealed stagehand hauled on a string and the star arose in the East, over the place where the baby lay.

It was exactly as the Good Book had foretold.

Meanwhile the shepherds had sneaked into their positions in the dark and lay ready. The Narrator's voice rang out clearly: "And, behold, there were shepherds in the fields, keeping watch over their flocks by night."

The Ford headlamp swung round to reveal a group of farm shepherds, each squatting next to a fine merino sheep tethered firmly to a peg in the lawn.

"And, lo, the angel of the Lord appeared unto them and they were sore afraid."

The shepherds, however, seemed anything but afraid, and were chatting together quietly about the braai that was to follow, when the angel of the Lord (my sister-in-law, Penny) stepped out from behind a pine tree.

She looked sternly at the shepherds, nudged the closest one with her toe and snapped out a curt order: "Skrik, julle!" (Be afraid, you lot!)

When they were finally afraid to her satisfaction – pointing in terror and exclaiming "Hau, Jonga!" (Gosh, look at that!) – the angel raised her white robed arms and said soothingly: "Fear not, for I bring you glad tidings of great joy."

At that moment the star in the east caught fire and was hurriedly lowered back behind the summerhouse where a quick-thinking member of the angel choir doused it with a watering can.

From across the tennis court came the clip-clop of hooves and the Three Kings appeared, magnificently mounted on farm horses draped in Persian rugs and following yonder star (which was now just a wooden box with a dark, five-pointed hole in it).

By far the most impressive was King Melchior, ably portrayed by Nzame Maliti on his specially bought Percheron horse. Nzame is a tall and imposing man at the best of times and on the ordinary farm horses his toes tended to drag on the ground. It had taken some serious searching to find a horse big enough for him. Even if it had just been for the play, it was worth it. In his golden robes and crown, seated on the giant white horse, he was positively dazzling.

All in all, the play proceeded smoothly to its close and after the final bow everybody agreed it had been a memorable experience and well worth the effort.

People had travelled from as far away as Hanover and Steynsburg, and everybody assured the team that the journey had been worth it. It was without any doubt the very best Christmas play they had ever seen.

So far there have been no offers from Hollywood, though.

Or from Oberammergau.

Spirits and Sad Places
(A sort of ghost story)

In the 1940s and '50s we knew exactly where the evil little tokoloshes lived because all the Xhosa farm staff told us about them.

Tokoloshes carried away children – and sometimes young women – and they were never seen again.

If you passed through the "Poort" late at night you took care not to stop there, and if your vehicle was a bicycle you just pedalled like mad and hoped for the best.

The Poort is a narrow break in the chain of low ironstone koppies, through which the Oorlogspruit River runs on its way to join the Gariep (Orange) River after a rain. There's always water in the river there and the spot has become known as the Fishing Pool.

Rumour has it there are fish in the pool, but nobody has seen any for many years. We used to fish there as kids, but all proper fishermen know that fishing has little to do with actual fish. It's all about collecting worms in the garden and finding the right sort of pole and hook and getting your mother to pack the right kind of sandwiches. It's all about long, dreamy afternoons in the shade of the sighing poplar trees that line the riverbank, while jewel-bright dragonflies skim the surface of the water. It's all about watching the hundreds of red bishop birds build their complex basketwork nests in the reeds overhanging the water.

The fishing pool is only a hundred metres or so from the Poort. It has none of the sadness of the Poort, though. As youngsters we could all feel the little tremor of evil when we walked through the Poort, even at midday.

Strangely, white adults couldn't feel the badness of the place and, as the staff became more sophisticated and acquired radios and TV sets and cars, they stopped bothering with the tokoloshes. A diviner from Somerset West once told me that young children and unsophisticated tribal people felt the presence of strange forces far more keenly than adults and those who had been brainwashed by so-called education into believing such things did not exist.

Just the other side of the Poort, about five kilometres from us, is the farm Oorlogspoort. Our closest neighbours lived here and had children about the same age as us.

We sometimes went over to visit them, but I never felt comfortable there.

We children once explored the old derelict farmhouse and found ourselves talking in whispers. Strangely, none of us suggested going back again, although a ruined old house would seem the ideal place for small children to explore.

I clearly remember my horror at seeing an ancient rotting ham swinging on a rusty chain in the kitchen chimney. Maybe that added to the eerie atmosphere.

I am told that the farm's name, Oorlogspoort (war ravine), refers to the fact that it was the site of the last of the "Bushman Wars" in the area.

Apparently the farmers grew tired of having their cattle and sheep stolen by the little Khoi people who lived in the mountains and regarded all animals as public property. To them, the idea of anybody "owning" an animal was absurd. You hunted what you required and it became yours once you had killed it. The farmers saw things differently.

So they formed a posse and drove the Khoi over the koppies and hunted them all to death. They called it a war, probably to give their brutality a veneer of respectability. Maybe the spirits of the slain Khoi live on in the Poort.

Whatever it is, the people of Oorlogspoort have not had a happy history.

There were three sons and a beautiful daughter of our generation there. The boys all died tragically while quite young. The daughter, Denise, was involved in a car accident and became a quadriplegic.

After the farm was sold the new owner – apparently prosperous and highly respected in farming circles – drove out into the veld one Christmas Eve and shot himself. A sad place.

Another place that frightened me as a child was my uncle's farm, Rooihoogte, in the Middelburg district. For no reason I could explain I felt threatened whenever I went there as a child. On two occasions I accompanied my father to Rooihoogte on partridge shooting weekends.

Both times I woke during the night and was messily sick.

The adults, of course, declared it was something I had eaten. I knew it was fear. But how do you tell that to an adult?

I remember one day walking across the high mountain ridge behind our house with my father. We descended on the far side and there, on a secluded little plateau, was a row of small earth mounds, hardly visible after years of wind and rain, but still there if you knew where to look.

He told me they were the graves of the last of the Bushmen.

I felt nothing there. No feeling of sadness or fear. The view was superb and the wind carried only the calm clear notes of birdsong. The mounds concealed no more than forgotten bones and dust.

The spirits were far away. Returned to the Poort where they belonged.

SIMUNYE - OR ARE WE?

There were Christmases when as many as fifty small black children, all dressed in their festive finery, would come down to the main house in the morning to sing their carefully rehearsed carols for my parents.

Singing played a big part in their lives, both at the little farm school they attended and also at home. Some were visitors: children of brothers or cousins who had come to spend the holidays on the farm. Most were the children of farm workers. After the singing there was always a great deal of identification.

"Now whose little girl is this?" Dad would ask. "I haven't seen her before."

"No, that's Tonkiyo's child. She's staying with us for Christmas. You remember Tonkiyo? He is October's youngest son, who left to join the police in 1958. He lives in Middelburg now."

My parents always bought great boxes of sweets from the local wholesalers before Christmas and these were distributed among the children, whose parents had made sure they came equipped with plastic shopping bags for the occasion.

After the singing and exchange of good wishes, the straggling line of children would make their way back to their houses, cheeks bulging, faces sticky and pockets filled with sweetness to come.

One recent Christmas morning Nzame and the other adult staff members came down to wish the family a happy Christmas as usual. There were no children this year and, for the first time, no carols. It was rather a sad moment and all of us – staff and family – stood together and remembered the old days of big families and real children's Christmases. Now the last generation of farm children had grown up and left to work in the cities, or to learn trades and professions.

"Maybe we should go back to the family planning clinic and ask them to let us make children again," said Nzame sadly, only half in jest.

Big families were a feature of Xhosa life until a few decades ago, and family traditions were different then.

In the rural areas families were extensive, close-knit groups and one of the fine traditions that have died is the giving of the first-born son to his grandparents.

There was a practical reason for this. Before the days of pensions or medical aid schemes, old people might well end up alone and in need of support at the end of their lives. So their first grandson was handed over to be raised by his grand-parents. It was not a real parting, because the real parents were always close by and obviously the natural mother would nurse the child while it was a small baby. But later his grandparents would become his parents and raise him as their own and he would be there for them, at the peak of his earning days, when they grew too old to look after themselves. Ignorant whites who didn't understand this fine tradition often regarded it with scorn, particularly in the cities.

"What do you mean you want two days off to attend your father's funeral? I remember you took a couple of days off six months ago to attend your father's funeral. You think I am stupid or something?"

And to the worker it was all rather confusing. Surely there was nothing unusual about having two fathers – one real father and a second one who was actually his grandfather, but accepted in the family as his father. Everybody had two fathers and two mothers. How could anybody not know that? Whites can be so dumb!

There were other Xhosa traditions that caused racial tensions.

In country communities you sat down on the ground when in the company of somebody you respected. It was right that he should be above you and look down on you. In the city office a worker might be called into the boss's office, where, to show his respect, he would immediately head for a chair and sit down, making himself as low as possible. It would be very rude to stand there towering over somebody who was your respected employer.

Many bosses regarded this traditional display of respect as exactly the opposite.

"That cheeky bugger! He walks in here and just sits down without being invited to, and slouches there as though he owns the place!"

Simunye, we say. We are one now. But there are still some wide chasms to be bridged before the oneness becomes a reality.

Keep Right on to the End of the Road

The Karoo is not a precisely defined area, but it is generally understood that it ends at the Orange River, now known as the Gariep River, a few kilometres north of Colesberg.

Here the great N1 highway crosses the river at a little settlement called Norval's Pont, and the wide grassy plains of the Free State begin.

John Norval, after whom the place was named, came to South Africa with the 1820 Settlers and must have drifted away from the Eastern Cape quite soon after his arrival. In 1839 he bought a farm called Dapperfontein on the banks of the Gariep River and settled there with his wife Mary Jane (née Murray).

There was a drift across the river at that point, but the crossing was often dangerous after rains, so the enterprising Norval built a pontoon, which he named the Glasgow, after his old hometown. Even in the middle of Africa, it seems, you can't keep a good Scot from building a ship.

This sturdy little craft was propelled by eight oarsmen and ferried people, animals and wagons across from one bank to the other.

Norval's Pont became such a popular crossing place that John built an inn on the riverbank nearby and called it the Glasgow Pont Hotel.

For many years this was a popular drinking spot for local farmers and passing travellers. I am told that the barman had strict orders never to have seen anybody when wives called to enquire whether they'd been there.

After some years of successful operation, the pontoon was washed away and found later, a few kilometres downstream. Two Norval boys were sent off to collect it and towed it back, using a team of oxen.

Soon after this John Norval handed over the running of the pont to his son James, who later had a bigger and better pontoon built in Colesberg and propelled by a team of men pulling on a cable stretched across the river. Operating the pont was an expensive business and, to ensure a steady stream of customers, James built a fine road all the way to Cradock and kept it in good repair. Records sent to me by Belinda Gordon of the Colesberg Museum show that the charge for the use of Norval's Pont was one pound for a wagon and slightly less for smaller vehicles.

When the river was too full for the pontoon to operate, a queue of wagons and carriages would form. On one occasion there were as many as five hundred vehicles lined up waiting for the pont crossing to be safe. It must have been a stirring sight.

When the railway line reached the Gariep River in 1890 an impressive rail bridge was built at Norval's Pont. It was considered the best bridge in all of South Africa, about five hundred metres long, with eleven huge columns of solid concrete. In 1900 retreating Boer forces blew up the bridge to prevent the British following them. Once more Norval's Pont was put to good use, ferrying materials across the river for the rebuilding of the bridge. During this operation the cable snapped and the pont capsized, drowning thirty people. Legend has it that a team of mules on the upturned pont became caught on one of the bridge piers by their harness and floated there, dead, for many days, presenting a macabre sight until the river subsided enough for them to be cut loose. The pontoon itself was found some miles downstream on the Free State side and returned once again to service.

Life is much less exciting at Norval's Pont today. The pont has long gone and a sturdy road bridge spans the river instead. Most travellers speed past with just a brief glance at the silver ribbon of water crawling below.

They leave the Karoo behind with little idea of the romance and history of the area through which they have passed. To them it's just a grey and rather boring stretch on the long road to civilisation.